Poems and Expressions

AuthorHouse™
1663 Liberty Drive
Bloomington, IN 47403
www.authorhouse.com
Phone: 1-800-839-8640

©2011 JADE. All rights reserved.

No part of this book may be reproduced, stored in a retrieval system, or transmitted by any means without the written permission of the author.

First published by AuthorHouse 3/21/2011

ISBN: 978-1-4389-3105-0 (sc)

Library of Congress Control Number: 2009902855

Printed in the United States of America

Any people depicted in stock imagery provided by Thinkstock are models, and such images are being used for illustrative purposes only.
Certain stock imagery © Thinkstock.

This book is printed on acid-free paper.

Because of the dynamic nature of the Internet, any web addresses or links contained in this book may have changed since publication and may no longer be valid. The views expressed in this work are solely those of the author and do not necessarily reflect the views of the publisher, and the publisher hereby disclaims any responsibility for them.

Dedicated to My Best Friend...And In Memory Of "Stimpy"

**Inspiration is someone...or something who can make you feel
that life can go on...regardless of the situation....and just because you have come
to the Winter of your life...doesn't mean you will never see another Spring.
Never give up on the dreams of your youth...Spring will surely come...
and with this fresh New Season...comes a rebirth of things we had once
thought were buried deep beneath Winter's cold...hard ground.
This is what Stimpy...My Pup...My Best Friend taught me about life...each and every time I would
look into his deep sullen eyes of Brown...I found the true meaning of the words "Best Friend."**

Jade

**In Memory of my Dad,
(James H. Stephens)
May, 1921 - March 1980**

**To My Dad... Though words have built this book that I dedicate to you, they cannot express my
gratitude enough. Thank you for nurturing my creative spirit, as well as my physical being.**

Table of Contents

TIMES ARE A-CHANGING 1

THE MUSIC ROOM 7

A PLACE IN HER HEART 10

TO HOLD A FLOWER IN YOUR HAND 12

A COZY LITTLE PLACE 15

I AM BLIND, BUT I CAN SEE 17

LEAVING WELL ENOUGH ALONE 20

YOU WON THE BET 22

OLD SOULS 24

WHO TURNED OUT THE LIGHT TO MY SOUL? 26

STANDING AT MY WINDOW 28

MOMENTS PAST GONE 30

ONLY TIME 33

IF THINGS WERE REALLY AS THEY SEEM 36

WHAT A WASTE 37

WHAT IS IT I'M LOOKING FOR? 40

THE IMPOSSIBLE DREAM 42

JUST SITTING HERE THINKING 44

SLEEP 47

BRAND NEW DAY 50

A LITTLE BIT 51

HERE I GO AGAIN 52

IT'S THE SONGS OF OLD 54

STANDING ON A HILLSIDE SO FAR AWAY 55

WHAT WAS THE CAUSE? 59

THEY MARCHED TOGETHER 63

AUTUMN 66

WINTER, WHITE RAIN 67

SPRING 69

SUMMER 71

THEY 73

A ROSE GREW IN A GARDEN ONE DAY 75

THE PUP AND THE PUSSYCAT 80

KINGO MY BUDDY, KINGO MY FRIEND 83

FROM MY HOME TO YOURS 87

INSPIRATIONS 89

THIS ONCE UPON A LIFETIME OF MINE 93

NOVEL LIVES, IN MY OPINION 95
NIGHTLY TRAVELS—EXPRESSIONS BY JADE 97
TO MY HEART I AM NO STRANGER 99

SPIRITUAL POETRY **101**

ONE SINGLE CANDLE AND A FLOWER 103
YOU ASKED ME TO PRAY FOR YOU 105
OH, WHERE WOULD WE BE WITHOUT PRAYER? 109
RIVER OF DESPAIR 111
DEAR HEAVENLY FATHER, IT'S ME AGAIN 114
STANDING IN THE DOORWAY OF TODAY 118
THANKS FOR THE BOUNTY 121
BABES IN CHRIST 125
A KIND WORD 127
AN ANGEL IN THE MAKING 129
AN ANSWER TO DONNIE'S LETTER 132
KIND WORDS FROM A STRANGER 134
REMEMBERING 136
HEAVEN'S SPLENDID SYMPHONY 138
YOU WERE THERE 141
ANGEL FRIENDS 143
HIS PICTURE 145
HE HAS RISEN 146
WHAT DO YOU SEE? 148
ANOINTING HANDS 150
ANGEL GIRL 152
JUST ONE MORE MILE WITH JESUS 154
HOW THE WEST WAS WON = (ONE) 155
LESS, OR A LOT, BUT NEVER ASK WHY 158
THE LOSS OF A CHILD 161
THIS TIME TOMORROW 163
TODAY 165

LOVE POETRY **169**

OH, IF ONLY 171
A ROSE AT THE END 174
WHEN HE SAYS "I LOVE YOU" 176
STANDING IN YOUR SHADOW 179
TO LOVE YOU WITHOUT A DOUBT 181

TO DANCE WITH YOU..183

A DAY THAT WILL LAST A LONG NIGHT'S TIME..186

AND THE MUSIC PLAYS ON 188

A SONG OF LOVE JUST FOR YOU 191

A LOVE LIKE THIS 193

THE KISS OF DEATH..195

WHO DOES YOUR HEART BELONG TO? 199

YOUR MEMORY...201

WHAT HAPPENED TO US? 203

AS I STILL THINK OF YOU, DO YOU STILL THINK OF ME? 206

I ALWAYS KNOW WHEN YOU'RE NEAR 209

DON'T BREAK MY HEART 210

YOU AND ME 212

ANOTHER DAY IN PARADISE..215

A LITTLE LOVING 216

FANTASY—YOURS OR MINE?..217

IMPRISONED BY YOUR WORDS 220

I LIKE YOU..224

I LOVE YOU, TOO 226

I NEVER KNEW 230

MMMM, TO KISS YOU 232

STOP YOUR CRYING, AND WIPE YOUR EYES 236

NO LAST CHANCE 237

WHEN THEY MET 240

I PAINTED YOUR MEMORY...243

vii

Welcome to all who enjoy the art of inspiration.
I have found that within each of us is a deep desire to express, in some form,
Our innermost thoughts
And feelings.
If I were an artist,
I would paint my poetry as I see it,
But that is not my gift.
So please enjoy what I have painted here with my mind's eye—
My words of inspiration and self-expression.

Jade

TIMES ARE A-CHANGING

"Times are a-changing," the old man thought to himself as he sat on the front porch of his old home place in the warm summer evening,

Watching the traffic as it passed,

Moving so fast,

Not like the years of long ago,

When all things seemed to move so slow.

So many memories crowding his now-trite mind,

Of all the old-fashioned times,

As he continued to sit there in his well-worn rocking chair,

With no lingering thoughts of tomorrow, for he no longer seemed to care.

"Yes sir, times are a-changing. Is this old world really going anywhere?"

As his mind continued to stare back into his vanished past,

Thinking, "What happened to the times when life wasn't moving this
fast?"

No one was in a rush to hurry up and slow down,

Rocking back and forth,

As he listened to the cracking of the well-worn rocker,

With his eyes closed and his head laid back against the top of the chair,

As though he just didn't seem to worry or care.

He glanced down at his old, tired, sun-worn hands,

And thought once again how hard he had worked all through his life,

To support his children,

And his now-deceased wife,

"What was it really all about?"

Reflecting upon those days when his now-tired body was always racked
with pain,

All he now found himself doing, in the winter of his life,

Was having daydreams of his children and his wife,

Of his youthful days.

Now all he seemed to be doing with what time he had left of his life,

Was just rocking it all away.

He listened in his memory to the haunting voices of children

As they played in the front yard,

And envisioned with his imagination,

As he heard himself yelling out loud,

"Don't bounce that ball too hard, John,

And watch out for your mama's flowerbed!"

The many shades of the wild flowers she would plant next to the house,

And the kinfolk would come by now and then,

And brag on her "green thumb."

Yes, those lovely old memories he could still see,

Even though time had come much too soon,

And took it all away,

But he would not allow time to flee,

For as he would always remind himself,

"This is one thing in this old life that no one can take away from me."

The old mulberry tree that now covered his entire porch with shade,

What a mess it would make,

But the shade it gave made it all worthwhile;

He remembered when he planted it,

His firstborn was but a small child.

But now times were a-changing,

And nothing looked the same;

Almost everyone he used to know,

Was now long gone,

And this made him empty,

And even more alone.

His children all grown,

With families of their own,

He did hear from them from time to time.

He realized they didn't understand what sadness and grief continued to
        beat in his old heart now.

He placed his hand over his heart,

And thought with a grin,

    "I wonder exactly how many times this old heart has continued to
        beat to keep this old shell of a body from falling apart?"

Well, another day had come to its end.

He stands from his resting place there in his rocker

And walks toward the screen door.

But this late evening, the moon was full and bright,

So he takes one last, long look at the open field across the highway,

So barren and infertile it all looked now,

"Things are a-changing, yessir, they surely are,"

As he shakes his head in despair of what was now considered the future,

And there once again was that familiar sadness in his heart,

As he wished he could somehow reach way back into the past,

And bring it all back the way it used to be for him—

The laughter of his children at play,

And the warm smile of his gentle wife,

And those days when the cost of living was only half the price.

He slowly opens the screen door,

And steps inside the house,

Something he had been doing for what seemed like all his life.

He looks at the clock over the fireplace mantel,

And his tired eyes slowly gaze upon the faces of his family in the old
picture frames that sat silently about the room.

He closes the door behind him,

As if he were closing out the world,

And fumbles for the latch,

Remembering once again a time when one could go to bed of an
evening,

Leaving the doors unlatched—but that time was so long ago now.

He makes his way into his now-empty bedroom,

Empty of anyone to share his long, lonely nights with,

Tucks himself into bed,

And with his memories drifting back and forth in his head,

He lays his head upon his well-worn pillow.

And as he lays there in the moonlit room,

He thanks God for what he had many years ago,

And as he was praying silently,

He drifted off into that eternal sleep.

Yes, indeed, "Times are a-changing"; from this life he did part,

But for all of his precious old memories,

They remained locked inside his now peaceful heart.

THE MUSIC ROOM

The *Baby Grand*,

A small piano,

Only about five feet long,

Still sits near the open bay window in the old, two-story house

That was once my childhood home.

With trembling fingers

And tiny hands

I watched from a distance this *Baby Grand*.

Its keys of ivory,

Keys black as slate,

In its lovely cherrywood case.

I watched as it continued to await the welcoming of our upcoming date.

Sitting there in the music room,

Waiting to come alive with its magic.

Classical tunes.

As strangers passed outside the window on the street below,

They would hear the tunes that seemed to shout a loud echo,

This echoing of the haunting sounds

That would float out of the window

And down to the silence of those standing around.

The *Baby Grand* would continue to play

All through the night

And all through the day.

Who was at the helm unlocking this *Baby* as it slept, with the keys that
would continue to beckon me?

(Even though I sat not upon the piano bench

And allowed not the music in my heart to be quenched.)

But I still continued to stare in the direction of this rare piece.

Even though it was a Baby,

It could become quite a beast.

A beast of majestic croons

That would fill all with the lust of its magical tunes.

I now look out

And to my amazement I find

A huge audience applauding the great symphony of my long-ago talents.

And as I continued to play with the thunder of the symphony's tunes,

I was yet that small child

In the music room.

A PLACE IN HER HEART

As she lay upon her bed all made of satin and lace,

She drifted as being borne along by the wind

To another time,

Another place.

A place where she had been many times in the past,

A time in her life

When it was blessed with happiness.

For she was once again with the ones she held dear to her heart,

And never did she give a thought for these precious times to part.

As she continued to lie there in her twilight slumber,

She drifted to those magic places of delectable wonder.

A smile was once again upon her soft face,

As soft as the pillow made with that same satin and lace,

For she was in that once-again mastery passions of a place.

Perhaps a place she never shared with others,

A perfect world that existed only beneath her covers.

Oh, so safe and secure she felt each time she would travel there,

Without one single worry or one single care.

But as her mind gently jolted her to a wakened state,

Her now sleepy eyes filled with warm tears.

For within her heart and within her mind

She realizes all those precious memories she left behind of that (long ago place

And that long ago time).

TO HOLD A FLOWER IN YOUR HAND

What do your eyes see when you hold a flower in your hand?

So gentle,

Like a small bird that would fly away.

To bring it up to your nose

And smell its certain scent,

It has to be *heavenly meant*.

To remember times that had passed,

And someone you love had given you a fresh, long-stemmed rose,

And you wished you could make that lovely rose last.

Never to dry up

And fade away,

Leaving only the memory of that special day,

To close your eyes and dream of all the lovely flowers that grow,

This is a memory within each of us that shall never grow old.

So what do you see in your hand

With that flower you hold?

How odd Mother Nature can be at times,

When we are not allowed to see the lovely flower's petals unfold.

They always seem to have their hint of color,

That flower we hold,

And the smell is already there when we bring it up to our nose.

Oh yes, the flowers, what a creation they are to behold,

For in each of them are the colors of a rainbow,

Some all the same,

And with each

They have their own name,

And, as with each of us,

None looks the same.

So I take these flowers as one of God's many tokens of love,

And I always give Him the glory for this gift,

For many hearts and spirits

These precious flowers will uplift.

A COZY LITTLE PLACE

Photos on the walls, a lamp on a table near the overstuffed chair,

That familiar smell of pipe tobacco fills the air,

And if I stand in the center of the room,

I can see you sitting there. A cherrywood coat rack next to the door,

Throw rugs scattered about the hardwood floors,

And a lovely view through the sliding glass doors,

A warm fire burning in the open fireplace.

If I close my eyes

I can feel its warmth upon my face,

Remembering you always saying to me,

"This little room is such a cozy little place."

I open my eyes,

And the room is bare. There are no photos on the walls,

No cherrywood coat rack next to the door,

No throw rugs scattered on the hardwood floors,

No lamp on a table near the overstuffed chair,

And no more familiar smoke tobacco filling the air.

And then it dawns on me once again as in many times past,

That *cozy little place* no longer exists.

It's just an empty shell of a house where you and I once dwelled.

The shared laughter,

And tears.

What happened to all those years?

Where did they all go?

I wish we could have them all back,

Everything the way it was,

Our dreams, our hopes,

And most of all, our love.

The photos on the wall,

A lamp on a table near the overstuffed chair,

And most of all that familiar pipe tobacco filling the air.

The room is not that *cozy little place* it used to be,

Simply because you're not here with me.

In Loving Memory of Nichole Boyd
(May 04, 1998–July 08, 2004)

I AM BLIND, BUT I CAN SEE

I am blind,

But don't feel sorry for me because I can smell all the things you can only see.

I can feel smiling faces looking at me; faces that have voices that make me giggle and want to play.

I can use all my senses that were given to me,

And I never take things for granted because I can't see.

My tiny hands grasp what I feel. I rub them to my rosy cheeks,

And lift them to my button nose, and there is nothing that smells as
lovely as this thing called a rose.

I can taste this smell that you can only see.

God in Heaven made these adjustments for me.

It is said,

We don't miss what we've never had.

So don't be sad for me, just be glad,

For I can touch your smile,

I can feel your frown.

So keep smiling when you look at me, and please don't say, "Poor little
child, she can't see."

'Cause even though I'm blind,

I am who God made me to be,

A three-year-old full of energy.

I have my bad days as we all do,

But I can still play and go to school.

There are others like me there.

We learn special things

And there is so much to share.

So please don't feel sorry when you look at me.

I may be blind, but I can see.

LEAVING WELL ENOUGH ALONE

This day shall pass away

And be no more,

Like a love who walks out of your life

With the slamming of the door.

But I see a new day on the morrow's horizon

A new range of old things, a chance for one's rebirth

As it is with each new day of our lives here on earth.

If we could have the chance to reach out

And grasp the world in our hands, I can't help but wonder

What would be my plans?

Would I rearrange the world to fit all of that which I do desire

And maybe just a few of the small things that I merely like?

Would I turn the day into one long night

So I could watch the stars so bright?

Would I take the time for others

And not just for me?

To look through their eyes, to see what they see?

Would I have compassion toward another's disposition,

Or would I just let them cause me more oppression?

How would I rearrange the heavens?

Would I turn one week into ten days instead of seven?

Would I think of others

And give them more time to ask forgiveness,

More time to forgive?

Or would all of this be totally against God's perfect plan for the heavens

And for Man?

So I guess if it's okay,

I'll just keep everything the same.

For I would have too much to lose

And nothing to gain,

For everything is perfect,

Just the way God intended it to be,

And the only thing that needs changing

Is just little 'ol me.

YOU WON THE BET

Descend into that place you've never been,

Just spread your arms wide

And close your eyes.

Spread your wings

And pretend to fly

Upward and upward toward the sky.

Now take in a deep breath now that you have arrived.

Open your eyes

And look down.

Beneath your feet you see or feel no space or ground.

You see that bright star in the heavens?

Looks as though you could reach out and grab hold.

You can.

Just stretch out your hand.

Don't be afraid.

You can do it.

Just remain calm and brave.

You have earned this chance,

So don't waste it.

You just can't,

Because if you do,

Nothing will ever be the same for you.

Such is how we live our life

With both feet planted firmly on the ground.

Know your goal in this life.

You never have to fly too high.

It's been right in front of you all this time.

And then, at the final end,

You can say, *Yesss!*

I made it once again.

I held that shining star right in my hand

And I made it back to earth again.

I found out that I could finally rise above all that was keeping me down."

So what if you took the gamble?

What's important is (*you won the bet*).

And for this you shall be rewarded

And never have any regrets.

OLD SOULS

The sand is hot beneath my burning feet,

Like the sands of the parched land of Eden,

Like the neglected plot of God's garden.

As my feet carry me many a long mile to reach into the past,

I cannot rest,

For my soul is old,

But my heart is yet young.

As I feel the heat bearing down on me,

As I continue to walk across this spartan, barren square of the desert,

To reach a time that I know awaits me,

My flesh is like that of a scaled fish.

I feel the pain so new,

But yet so familiar to this heart,

As I have many miles to tarry before I find you once again

To fill my heart.

Don't move now from your place of standing,

Wait for my return.

I will walk during the heat of the day

And follow the path of the sun.

And when the night closes in

And the sands of this desert shine like the moon

My journey will end again.

Again the morning will come and I will reach you soon,

So wait for this love of long ago.

This body is young,

But this soul is old.

WHO TURNED OUT THE LIGHT TO MY SOUL?

I grab my coat from off the hook

And open my door

And step out to take a look.

Oh, the crispness of the fall morn

Is now fully born.

I see the many colors of leaves as they fall

And gently make their way to the cold ground.

I can smell winter in the air

As the clouds above turn a darker shade of gray.

I now realize summer has been put to rest and soon will come the snow.

As I pull the door closed behind me with a slam

And step out onto the dampness of the cold ground,

And I walk to the edge of my yard,

And turn to look around,

I see nothing but a memory of when I was a child.

And *So where did I just step from?*

Came a thought to my soul.

Who turned out that eternal flame?

Of all the yesteryears that no longer remain.

I shuffle down to the sidewalk that ran across my mind,

And start my long walk back from that long ago time.

Within my heart, my youth will forever remain,

And to this past I shall reframe,

Taking with me only the good that will forever sustain.

Oh, the sweet precious memories of so long ago. For I now realize I am
    a ghost,

Searching for my soul.

STANDING AT MY WINDOW

I stand in the doorway of this new day, looking out my window at
       tomorrow,

Praying for peace instead of sorrow.

A bird comes and lands on my window's ledge.

Two more soon follow,

And now there are three.

I gently sprinkle a few breadcrumbs on the window's ledge,

Not wanting them to flee,

As I listen to them sing a gracious thank you to me.

Oh, the sounds of the day,

How I love them so,

Standing at my window,

Not wanting to let go.

For such precious moments,

They never seem to last,

They belong to yesterday,

Which will soon become our past.

The purpose of our future has yet to be told,

Only with each second can we see our lives unfold.

We cannot change what happened yesterday,

The good nor the bad,

But we can hang onto all the good things

And bury all the sad.

So I will stand at my window

With each new day that dawns

And listen to the birds as they sing my favorite songs.

I will ring in each new day

As we do each New Year

By raising up my cup of coffee with a toast of good cheer:

"Here's to today,

And all that it may bring,

Standing at my window hearing the birds sing."

MOMENTS PAST GONE

As I sit and look across the span of time that crosses that space of yours
and mine,

That space we hid within each of our minds.

I can't help but wish that all of my memories were that of a wonderful
time,

But as we both can relate

That moment in time came much too late

And to each of us

We let that perfect time escape.

Oh, how I wish dreams did come true,

For if they did

I would wish for that moment in time to have been different for me

And for you.

Speaking for myself,

That time that I am now spending

Would not exist.

I could have climbed those mountains of life; you know the kind I am
speaking of,

They hold no strife or malice,

Only mountains with much happier paths,

That we could have climbed,

Mountains with no deep valleys of the regretful kind.

I still can remember all those years since past, of special moments past
        gone,

Leaving us only the presence of our old home,

That place in our hearts,

That place in our minds,

That place of a much sweeter time.

Where did the time flee for you and for me?

Those precious moments past gone.

As I was plundering today among your many old things,

I came across this gold and ruby ring,

And I couldn't help but remember when I first gave it to you.

The look on your face

Was that of such a formal grace,

And then you placed a kiss upon my lips

And gave to me a warm embrace.

You did try to hid the look of surprise,

But my young heart knew what you were feeling inside.

An attic

And an old wicker chest,

Filled with warm memories of you

And of me,

Moments of your sweetness bring tears to my eyes

As I continue to look at our history inside.

If I could turn back the pages of time,

I often think, "What page would I turn to of our lives

And of those moments past gone?"

Would it be to the very beginning of time?

No!

I don't think so,

For it took too much of our time,

Time that could have been spent putting all that getting to know you far
behind.

I think I would have to turn to that page when we both knew the true
meaning of love,

That special time in both our lives when we grew to know that love was
merely a word

If left unexpressed,

And it only means love

As we both grew to know that it counts in the hearts and souls when two
can freely express

And two can freely show

(*Moments past gone*) of years long ago.

ONLY TIME

She was living a life of sorrow and shame,

It was not really her fault,

She wasn't to blame.

She was a model,

A young, pretty little thing.

She would wear the clothes,

She would do the walk,

She would contend with the stares from strangers who would admire the
lovely clothes she would wear.

She changed her hairstyle

For others to approve.

Her poor young life was always on the move.

She would starve herself to stay slim and trim.

(*Only Time*) brought her to this place and

(*Only Time*) could take her home again.

Where was home now?

For the show must go on.

A model's life is not their own.

(*Only Time*) was in control now and she knew she had to escape it some way,

Somehow.

She longed for those times of before,

Before her life was consumed by others.

She longed to be back home.

But once again,

(*Only Time*) could be her enemy,

Or her friend.

So one evening after the final walk down that long platform, all dressed in a long black gown,

She knew that this would be her last stage call.

No more doing what others had commanded her to do,

For she had lived that life of a foolish model

And that of a fool.

(*Only Time*) was waiting for her when the show came to a close,

And she ran to the dressing room

And ripped off her clothes.

"Now it is my turn to live," she said to herself, and took her old suitcase down from the closet shelf,

Packed the old things that were not fancy attire,

But it was who she was

And (*Only Time*) was her friend now.

As she walked out the door of the dressing room

And into the street she did go.

A loud thump was the last sound that was heard,

And as her thin,

Tired body lay there in the crowded street,

Someone came and covered it with a white sheet.

(*Only Time*) ran too fast

For this one to keep.

IF THINGS WERE REALLY AS THEY SEEM

From the very beginning we all have dreams,

Dreams of how we hope our lives will be.

And sometimes as we continue to grow,

We carry those unfulfilled dreams deep within our souls.

Then slowly times passes like the rush of the waves onto the seashore,

And we continue to dream just a little more.

And with age come changes,

Like stepping through an open door:

We grab onto the handle

And walk into the unknown,

Just with our dreams and plans we've created on our own.

But,

The dreams we dream can only come true if you will allow them to,

For no one will knock upon your door of life

And hand all those dreams to you.

Go out there in this big *'ol* world,

Get acquainted with what you don't know,

For knowledge is the key,

It can open a world full of magic and marvelous things,

But you are the only one who can make those things what they only in
the beginning turn into really what they seem.

WHAT A WASTE

We spend our youthful lives thinking, sometimes, about growing old and
      dying,

And we are more self-destructive then,

More than any other time in our lives,

And we're just too young to know any better.

Then there comes a time in our life when we feel as we look back on our
      youth,

We think to ourselves,

"Well, I got past that time."

But I am finding that death is no longer my enemy,

But just an unknown part of life,

And we start to drop that fear of death and dying.

Moving on in life,

Like a whirlwind, time seems to speed up rapidly for us,

And then before you have time to stop and catch your breath,

You are in what some may refer to as a "Midlife Crisis."

You can't go back,

You can't stay in that same era of time,

So you have no choice but to keep trudging on.

And at times you feel you would welcome death

Because you have only your youthful memories to look back on.

And even those good *memories* can become a soiled spot in our minds.
Why?

Because they always have a way of making us realize all of that precious
time had been such a waste.

We didn't have as much time to do all the things we felt we were meant
to achieve.

There just wasn't enough time

And I guess we are trying to be twenty

And always going on forty-nine,

A rut to say the least,

Spinning out of control.

And then one day,

You look in the mirror

And see that you're really getting old

And time is starting to move once again.

For we realize that *time*

Is no longer our friend.

So what is left when you're stuck in the middle of then and now,

And the only way out is but one of two choices?

You can get on with living,

Or you can get on with dying,

But we know that *dying* is close enough as it is.

We have to learn to *accept that which we cannot change*,

And be thankful that we have had more time to live than some we may know.

Don't waste one more precious moment.

Be happy and glad in the state you have found yourself in

And stop wasting that time for the end.

Today you were just born,

And no matter what your age may be,

Always look forward to tomorrow

And open your eyes each morning you awake

And grab onto living and give life a firm handshake—

Because you have come this far.

WHAT IS IT I'M LOOKING FOR?

What is it I am looking for

And can never seem to find

Or see?

It feels like there is something missing deep inside of me.

Could it be just memories of yesterdays long gone?

Is this feeling that I'm feeling because I feel so sad

And so alone?

I keep waiting for a miracle,

Perhaps, to come my way.

Whatever it is that I keep looking for

Must be a very

Long way away.

I guess that I'll just continue to look from day to day

For whatever it is I'm looking for to come my way.

And when the time is right,

It won't pass me by

Because whatever I'm looking for,

It has not yet arrived.

However, I do not enjoy this discontentment that I find myself in.

I can think of many other ways

I wish my days could be spent.

So I have no other choice

But to be happy in the state I'm in. Others may be happy and

Content with what they have each day,

But I guess, when it comes to me,

I'm different that way.

THE IMPOSSIBLE DREAM

Yes, I do suppose I have "dreamed the impossible dream" a time or two,
      but that is a foolish saying,

For those dreams never did come true,

And they didn't take me anywhere I wanted to go.

This distance I've traveled in this one life alone,

I could not even count, for the miles

Have only left me tired

And weary when it was all said and done.

Life is an *impossible dream*,

And those words mean more than what is truly known,

Those *impossible dreams*

Are only a bunch of poppycock,

For if you wait for those dreams to come true,

You will be the one who ends up being a fool.

I have burned bridges behind me,

That I can never cross again.

I have seen things with my eyes that I should have never seen.

I have been places that I shall never pass again.

I've cried tears that were all in vain.

I have loved,

But was never loved the same.

I've learned that even though I am an American,

It's not the *Land of the Free and the Brave*,

And the only real place in your heart that you can call home

Will be in your own grave.

I got on this train of life,

And I rode it to the end of the tracks.

And now that it has finally come to a stop,

I shall never look back.

And when someone tells you to "Stand up and be counted,"

You may as well remain seated,

Because when all the votes come in, they will never be honestly tallied.

Now I am sure there will be a few who will think I have a negative way
of viewing life,

And I do suppose this would be true,

But I am who I am,

And I can never be you.

So, my friend, you dream that impossible dream, and when you finally
wake in the end,

You will realize you're still where you've always been.

JUST SITTING HERE THINKING

Just sitting here thinking. Better than being someplace drinking

And making my mind all crowded.

Sitting here,

Watching the sun go down,

With all this weight I have bearing down on my mind— gets mighty
     heavy all the time.

I'm someplace I don't wish to be,

But it just so happens God made only one of me.

My body is one place,

This heavy heart is in another, and all my soul feels

Is trouble, trouble, trouble.

I sometimes wish that I could grow wings and fly,

With my wings spread wide,

Feeling that freedom inside.

I would fly to that place I wanna be,

That place where I can just be *me*.

And where would that place be? one might ask.

And I would have to answer, "A place I can't return to,

For it is a place from my past."

So I sit here watching the sun going slowly down,

Wasting my time

Because so much of my past still haunts my mind.

Oh, I do suppose we all have those moments when certain memories cast
their shadows across our minds,

But wouldn't it be wonderful if this time we waste

Could be directed into a more constructive place?

If we had no bad memories

Of yesteryear's time,

What then would we exactly have on our minds?

For tomorrow has not yet arrived,

For the good things in life we all need to strive.

So close that curtain that covers all those memories in your mind

And let them be put to rest.

As though it were the sun that slowly dips its mind into the west,

Put those memories to rest.

For tomorrow a new day will dawn,

And yesterday's frets will be gone,

And just maybe we may realize we're happy just being that one single
one.

SLEEP

How did I become this being that these tired eyes are seeing each time I
    look in the mirror?

Fog covered, dripping down the mirror—it strains my memories.

Dim lights with no glow,

I have to assume it is the presence of my getting old.

What happened to my youth?

Where did it go?

Perhaps it is still hiding there somewhere that I do not know,

In the mirror I have yet to know.

Sighs, cries, sorrows of so long ago

Still haunt my barren soul, dreaming dreams of those who have no faces,

Coming to me now in the darkness of my dreams to tell me good-bye,

Not knowing exactly why

As I wait for an answer.

I look for a sign

And then I hear the ringing of the phone.

And there on the other end

I hear the dreaded news of a loved one that has died.

Yet another has been taken from my life.

Never to look upon their face again, as I did in the many years now
faded.

I think now to myself,

Not many more are left that I know.

I feel stolen grief,

Sadness, and all I want to do now is (SLEEP) this time away.

I feel anger,

Rage within, because I had to wake from my (SLEEP).

I just want to wish all of this away.

But I realize I must stay in this damnable life.

Oh God, I pray every day, just let me (SLEEP).

I do not wish to be awake

And feel the craving of what I had taken for so long to mask this, all my
inner pain.

Just (SLEEP),

Sweet, peaceful (SLEEP), when I can no longer feel all of the pain inside
my heart

And mind,

Or remember no longer.

Sometimes I am awakened by another from a bad dream

That I do not even recall.

"What was this dream about?" they sometimes ask.

But I cannot remember.

I'm tired once again,

So now I must (SLEEP), for I do not wish to live and be wakened from
this sweet peace.

Sleep is now my only refuge. Time passes as I (SLEEP).

Just maybe, when I awake once again,

This time will have come to its final end,

Not this time that I am now in.

(SLEEP),

Sweet nights and days of slumber.

BRAND NEW DAY

I step out into this brand new day as all my days begin this way.

I go through the motions—

Those that are placed before me this day

As it plods along on its merry way.

Not much I can do,

Not much I can say,

I just have to make it through,

Stay on the correct course

And do not stray.

Things waiting to happen

Make me wanna run away to a place where I do not have to be so
        repetitious in all I do,

In all I say.

And then I think to myself,

"Tomorrow will be brand new,

And just maybe I will have the wonderful pleasure of meeting you."

A LITTLE BIT

I saw this paper and pen just laying there at the end of the table where
        you always sit,

So I decided to pick it up

And write (A Little Bit).

It is moments like these when I feel at ease within the silence where I sit,

And it is this strange silence that inspires me to write

(A Little Bit).

However, I must admit,

Even though I find the silence,

And to this I must submit,

I just love sitting here alone and writing (A Little Bit).

Now the words don't always come out as I had planned,

For there are those crazy moments when my mind cannot connect to the
        pen I hold within my hand,

So here I sit alone writing just (A Little Bit).

HERE I GO AGAIN

Yes, here I go again,

Same old feeling of not knowing where I belong.

Seems this "same old feeling" has haunted me for so long,

This emotional, empty feeling I feel deep inside,

It just won't let me live life on the outside.

The *outside* of me that I show to very few,

For that part of me that is myself

I keep hidden inside.

I feel at times I wanna unzip this body of mine

Step out of it and feel life the way I know it does exist,

For there is so much of it that I feel I have missed.

It seems no matter where I go,

Or whom I am with,

This damned feeling won't let me live.

So I wander around in that state of mind,

From room to room,

And stand at the window

And look outside.

And to think I could be one of the many people I see as they pass by,

And it is then I start to cry.

But no one sees my tears,

For they are like the rest of me:

I keep them buried deep inside.

I stand there

And say a silent prayer

And think to myself,

"My life is going nowhere." Is it depression? Or perhaps it is
   oppression.

All I know is that I find in my heart desperation.

Oh, my friends and family do not know who I am any longer,

For that part of me could not remain stronger. I became weak with too
   many unreal thoughts to ponder.

"Please let me out,"

My soul cries, but I ignore the whimpering sighs,

Hanging on by a thread,

For I know if this state of mind continues,

I will surely end up dead.

But what is one to do

When you break through

And you know what you're feeling is not you?

IT'S THE SONGS OF OLD

It's the songs of old that never grow old,

They always leave a memory of a special time and place.

Riding along in your automobile with the stereo on,

All at once you hear your favorite

Long-ago song,

And you reach to turn the music up

And start to sing along.

No matter how long is has been

Or when you heard the words,

They seem to come back to you as if it was still *then*.

And you have a big grin

Just because you still remember when.

So no matter what they may play today,

Tomorrow it will become a part of history.

Ahhh, yes!! Those old songs will never die—

They will continue to live longer than you or I.

STANDING ON A HILLSIDE SO FAR AWAY

The weather was calm,

But the humidity was high as I stood on that hillside watching the choppers fly by.

I think to myself,

I was a young man when I came to this place.

It has only been a year since the youth was removed from my face.

I was a man before no time at all,

Made to survive,

Be proud,

Stand tall, with my head held high,

My stomach tucked in,

No smile on my face,

Not even a grin.

My young eyes have seen what no eyes should see,

My mind won't give me peace

Or set my bad memories free.

For there is not a day

The face of death I do see.

A memory of a face that could have been a friend,

If not for this war we find ourselves in.

You can only be there as they are for you,

No close friends, for that would never do.

For at any moment

Death may come

And take them from you.

This foreign country we find ourselves in—

There is no place to run,

There is no place to hide. You have but one chance to live,

And but one to survive.

It doesn't look that bad from where I'm standing right now,

But soon I will join the rest of the troops. We're only numbers formed
        into groups.

With camouflage clothing

And army boots,

With rifles in our arms,

And gear on our backs,

Like a wide train on an endless track.

The choppers are landing now; they are calling my name, as I think to
        myself,

"I must be insane

Being in a war that I know nothing about,

Living in fear day in

And day out.

Fear grips my body

As I turn and walk away

From standing on that hillside so far away.

I have only this moment.

I must treat it as my last.

The morning is over,

And soon this day will pass.

I catch up with the troops

And fall in as I am told,

Marching to a rhythm like a song that is old.

I now hear the rounds

As they are being fired.

"Snipers are hiding in the bush up ahead.

We have six men wounded

And more are dead."

My body grows numb,

Even though we have been told.

One never hears the bullet that claims one's soul.

WHAT WAS THE CAUSE?

As the young soldier lay on the cold damp ground, his young life ebbing away,

What were the thoughts that rushed through his mind?

Were they the thoughts of his last day?

Were they of his family,

So far away?

His body all dirty,

His clothes were a mess,

But that didn't matter.

Who cared how he was dressed?

His buddies gathered 'round him,

With fear on their face,

Thinking "That could be me there in his place." His sergeant steps
forward

And leans down to hear the last words of the young soldier:

"What was our purpose for being here?"

As tears filled the eyes of those still gathered 'round,

They watched their buddy's blood soak into the ground. What could they
say to this dying young man? "Some words of encouragement
are needed here,

So hang in there, buddy,"

Came a cry from the crowd.

"Don't die like this; stand tall, be proud."

"Oh, leave him alone," came a low voice from the rear.

"Take off his jacket,

Remove his gear. He's fought a good battle

That no one will win.

It's time to let go,

He's met his end."

The dying young man gave a sigh of relief,

60

And a smile crossed his face

As he met his final sleep.

His now lifeless body was lifted from the ground

By the few who were still gathered around.

But the blood he shed

Lay soaking in the ground. "The battle is never over," another one cried.

"There is much more to come.

But for our buddy,

It's already done."

One might say, "What a waste that was

For such a young man to shed his blood."

But to him,

It was not a waste, as one could tell by the smile on his face. He fought a
    good battle

And he won the race,

Because he knew in the end

His purpose, his place.

So to all the young soldiers,

And the old alike,

Who have been sent to war

And stood up to fight,

World, stand up,

Take notice,

Know what it was for. There is never a winner when it comes to war.

The enemy,

The soldiers from our country's land,

Whoever they may be,

A child is a child,

And a man is a man,

But what makes us all equal

Is the freedom we believe in.

THEY MARCHED TOGETHER

As a family of brothers,

(*They marched together*) into the battlefields of hell, blinded by the rain that would sting their cold, muddy faces like a million scorpions. It was worse than they could have ever imagined,

But there was a war waiting, and all the brothers had to go and fight.

When the word *brothers* was mentioned, it did not mean as a brother in the real life,

But *brothers* who had been brought together to fight.

One meant as much to the other

As they did to them all.

No matter the size,

They were all men who stood tall and strong above us all.

The whistle had been blown,

And they all were called,

And as for the color of their skin,

They all fit in.

Some were going where others had already been.

(*War*) was the state they were now in.

So for the colors of the Red, White, and Blue,

(*They all marched*) together for me and you.

Oh, what a sight to behold

On that battlefield I did see,

For all the blood they shed for our country.

And if you look toward the east to this very day,

You will see the brothers. (*They marched together*) for you and for me
        and for the whole damn country.

I may not have known them personally,

But what they did for our country

Made me feel like I was a part of them.

And even to this very moment

The *war* continues on,

And we wait and pray for our brothers to come home.

AUTUMN

Autumn is the beginning birth of winter with all its golden color,

And splendor,

September, October, November,

And then comes December.

It takes all the seasons to make up this one,

They may take their time to arrive one by one,

But when we walk outside on that first,

Fresh crisp morn,

We then realize winter will soon be born.

It may be only sweater weather at this time of year,

Just a small reminder that winter is near.

The changing of the colors of the leaves on the trees,

And the cooler breeze is the only reminder that we need.

I can smell the crispness in the air,

And it makes me more anxious for winter to get here.

Yes, autumn is a part of it all,

Winter, spring, summer, and fall.

WINTER, WHITE RAIN

When the winter comes

And the howling winds blow,

I stand at my window

And watch the cold winter snow.

It's hard to believe that the flowers that were once there

Have suddenly disappeared, it seems, into thin air.

The leaves on the trees have all fallen to the ground.

Nothing looks the same.

Everything is now covered with what I call *white rain*.

It sticks to the windows,

The rooftops as well.

It can be a real mess,

But there is something about it everyone seems to love.

Christmas in the winter:

There is nothing that can compare

With the twinkling of the lights against all that white,

As the snow falls

And makes all so bright.

Smell coming from my kitchen

Of cookies being baked,

And the family gathered 'round

Waiting for a taste.

Inside the house

You feel cozy and snug as a bug in a rug.

Oh, the *white rain*,

I do love it so.

But it is because of the lovely white snow,

However, that I do look forward to the spring.

So I guess what it all comes down to is simply this:

None of the seasons

I would wanna miss

Because, no matter what

Winter, spring, summer, fall,

What can I say?

I love them all!

SPRING

Winter has been put to sleep once again. Now it is time for spring to
    awaken.

Everything that had been covered by the snow

Is unveiled by the spring to show all the lovely new growth that had been
    sleeping below.

It is like turning a page in a book,

From one season to the next.

It shows new, awesome wonders of what is to come forth next.

The trees sprout new leaves

And the tulips spring forth from their resting place in their bulbs

With an array of bright yellows, along with all the other lovely and
    unusual flowers.

The grass is green once again,

And sometimes it is so lovely,

We can't believe all that we're seeing.

We stand,

And gaze all around

At the beauty before us

And take in a deep breath and think to ourselves

Just how grand the springtime can be

And give a silent prayer in our hearts

That God has given us yet another year to behold all the beauty He has created for us to see.

SUMMER

I would love to have you come

And sit on my front porch swing with me,

Because my front porch is a peaceable place to be,

With all the many flowers in full bloom,

And huge wicker pots,

It seems to be the perfect spot.

Roses in my front yard,

Roses in the back,

Baby birds in the homemade birdhouses

Make one realize summer is surely awake.

Honeysuckle's growing on a trellis over five feet high.

One can't help but smell its lovely fragrance as they pass by.

Neighbors passing in front of my place,

Waving to me

With friendly smiles on their face.

A gentle breeze blows across my front porch

In the late afternoon.

It makes my front porch

My favorite place.

Just the two of us,

You and I just passing time

As it passes us by,

As we swing to and fro,

Drinking a cool glass of homemade lemonade.

Under the roof of my front porch

Is the perfect shade.

Oh, how I wish summer could last forever.

But then again, I look forward to the fall.

But (*summer*) will always be my most favorite season of all.

THEY

They were just two white horses. They traveled night and day. They fell in love in that same old usual way.

They were always together. They stayed together night and day. They never thought to stray.

They vowed to always remain this way. They roamed the wide-open plains. They climbed mountains together.

They kept driving with desire even in the sleet,

Snow, and rain.

They never did once complain.

They grazed the pastures, luscious and green.

They were the prince and the queen.

They slept under the stars so bright.

They would awaken each morning with the early light.

They lived life to the fullest,

Never dreaded one single day,

For they knew in their hearts they would always remain (they).

They cried tears of joy together

And in their special way I guess they prayed.

I got to know (they).

And how odd the names were to me,

For two white horses to share the same name.

For when you would call for one,

(They) both came.

Yes, (they) were special and different in this God-given way

For as I look into my past of long ago,

I will always wonder where did (they) go?

A ROSE GREW IN A GARDEN ONE DAY

A rose grew in a garden one day.

It was not like others,

It was different in so many gorgeous ways.

It stood out among all the rest—

Perhaps in the manner in which it had grown,

It was the very best.

Its colors were not that of an ordinary rose,

Not your typical garden-variety,

For anyone that looked upon this rose could see it was a rarity.

It received just the right amount of sunshine,

Just the right amount of rain.

And just the right amount of care

Surely didn't make it the same.

As the seasons came

And the seasons went,

This rose never seemed to change,

It did not go into its dormant stage.

However, its color did turn to gold

And everyone who saw it called it *the Golden Rose.*

And then one day a stranger came

And stole the rose away—

Extracted it from its special spot,

Took it away and crammed it into a small flowerpot.

Soon the Golden Rose felt stifled with no room for its fragile roots to
     grow,

It was no longer that same happy Golden Rose.

It seems to have a mind of its own—

And each day as it grew weaker, it would dream of being home,

The home where it was admired by all who would see its glimmer and
     its shine.

But this person who stole it from its happy place

Did not know what to do to bring its luster back.

So they covered it with a brown paper sack

And set the Golden Rose near a wooden fence out back.

A young boy came along

And opened this sack,

Thinking it had been tossed in the trash.

So he lifted it up and strung the heavy sack across his young back,

And carried this Golden Rose to his old worn place

Most would call an ugly shack.

The boy lived alone,

He had no family.

He had managed to survive on the streets for most of his young life. He
owned nothing of any value,

And he knew he and this rose had much in common.

So he took the now-dying rose

And placed it in his garden with gentle care.

After planting it there

He stood back and looked at it,

And then he said a silent prayer.

"Dear God in heaven,"

He continued to pray,

"I ask that you spare this flower

And let it bear,

Let it spring forth with new life once again,

As I know and believe it was lovely in the beginning,

I promise to nourish it with gentleness and care."

Well, as the weeks went by,

The young boy didn't let this Golden Rose die.

He did what he promised God he would do.

The Golden Rose made it through the winter,

Spring, and fall,

And so did the young boy

Who had faith through it all.

And soon this Golden Rose was lovelier than before,

And it remained in that small garden for many years to come.

The young boy grew into a young man

And with the Golden Rose became the best of friends.

Strangers would pass by

And admire this odd and gorgeous Golden Rose.

The young man died at a very young age, but before he passed

He had left in a will

His last wish:

He wanted to be buried in the garden with the Golden Rose at his head,

For the life of this rose, he knew, would forever remain,

For the gold in a rose

Was this boy's dream,

For it was as close to riches as he would ever be.

That same Golden Rose remains there still

And I suppose it always will,

For that Golden Rose was only a dream

And it could never be real,

For the things in this life

We know don't really exist

Can only come in movies

And dreams

And fairytales.

THE PUP AND THE PUSSYCAT

"Calm down,"

Said the puppy to the very upset cat.

"What in the world makes you act like that?

I promise I won't harm you,

I'll even wager you that bet.

So come down from those places that you run and hide from me,

For I am just a puppy,

That is very plain to see."

So the very timid pussycat

Sat there upon the kitchen counter top,

Looking down at the puppy

As he continued to bark.

"No," explained the pussycat to this very hyper pup.

"I would rather remain right here upon this counter top.

For you see, little fellow,"

The pussycat continued to explain,

"You are still but a puppy

And for this you are not to blame.

Even though I have been here long before you arrived,

I have no intention of giving up one of my nine lives.

So please shut up that loud barking

Before the police are called,

And off to the dog pound we shall both be hauled.

And my attention you will not get,

Even though you are a cutie,

To this I must admit,

But your barking I shall not let bother me one bit.

So just be patient

And please be quiet.

There is no need not to be polite.

For the masters of the home

Shall be returning before noon,

And this I am going to assume,

You're a spoiled little puppy, who wants his own way,

All because you wanna play.

But you see, little pup,

I am too tired for this.

I was not left here with you to indulge in your games,

And your barking is driving me insane.

So once again I do declare,

Please shut up and go hide somewhere.

For I am a feline:

Furtive,

But smart,

And I will not continue to listen while you continue to bark,

As I lay up here on this cool countertop."

KINGO MY BUDDY, KINGO MY FRIEND

I tiptoed into your room tonight

And stood at the foot of your bed watching you sleep.

You looked like a small angel lying there all tucked in,

And I was hoping to myself that you were dreaming happy and fun dreams.

I could see you running in an open field,

Learning how to fly your first kite,

Hearing you giggle, and seeing that smile on your face,

Or maybe you were dreaming of your first puppy, Kingo,

That outgrew you much too soon,

And then one day he was taken from you.

The angels swept down from heaven and lifted him up,

Or at least that is what I always told you.

"Kingo my buddy, Kingo my friend,

Don't fly too high in that terrible wind," you would say

As the tears streamed down your tiny cheeks

And landed on my breast as I held you close when you cried,

And I gently took my fingers and wiped your eyes.

And you looked up at me, and smiled,

Trying to reassure me that all was going to be okay,

As if you thought my heart was broken in the same way as was yours.

Oh, quite a little man you are.

I move closer to your bed to make sure you are covered and breathing
        okay,

As I did when you were but an infant,

As I would spend hours watching you sleep,

Not wanting you to slip away from me.

But I can see how time

Will soon take that child away and exchange it with a man,

And I feel the tears running down my cheeks.

I never want you to go away from me

Because the memories will never be enough to hold onto in this lifetime.

But you are my little man for a season.

And soon the spring of your life will arrive,

Bringing with it all the new adventures that you have yet to follow.

And then one day,

You will be sitting beside my bed,

Holding my hand,

And looking upon the face of an old woman

Who has come to the winter of her life

And will soon fade as so did my time in your youth.

I reach down

And gently brush your hair from your face,

And place a kiss on your forehead,

And whisper in a soft, low voice to you,

"Sleep sweet, my little angel,"

And turn and tiptoe out of your room,

And with a deep sigh

I hold onto this moment,

Not wanting it to pass me so quickly,

But knowing in my heart I have you with me for at least the time God
        allows for this moment now,

And this gives my soul comfort.

And I hum a silent tune,

"Kingo my buddy, Kingo my friend,

Don't fly too high in that terrible wind."

FROM MY HOME TO YOURS

I would like to take this time to wish you and yours a very Happy
Thanksgiving.

And if we stop for just a few seconds

And think really hard,

We can all find so many things to be thankful for.

I would also like to say my heart goes out to all the families who will
be remembering their loved ones who will not be sharing this
Thanksgiving with them,

But you will be remembering the many happy Thanksgivings that have
passed.

To you I express my deepest sympathy

And empathy for your loss.

As the tradition of Thanksgiving continues:

The turkeys will be baking, the pies will be made

In that same old family tradition, in that same old family way.

Guests will be arriving,

The tables will be set,

But the memories of our loved ones

We shall never forget.

So when you are all gathered together for this Thanksgiving feast,

And every head is bowed in prayer, remember in your hearts that
Thanksgiving is meant to be shared.

And though our loved ones may not be there to share in this
Thanksgiving feast, let's not forget to pray for peace.

INSPIRATIONS

"What inspires you?"

Someone recently asked me

And this was my reply to their question. I would have to say that I am
    inspired by the simple things in life,

Not the materialistic matters,

Which seem to collect into a huge bonfire within us.

I love the euphoria of life

Without it being drug induced.

We all seem to have those special moments in life

When our inspirations inundate us to the fullest.

We feel we must share these inspirations with others,

Like that of a revelation within our own souls,

That great divulgence.

I would have to expound at this time on the many inspirations I have
        received from being a lifelong resident of Florida,

And spending most of my life near the ocean;

Taking a stroll in the wee hours of the morning,

Listening to the ocean's loud roar

As though it were announcing to me, "Hey, this is a brand new day.

Enjoy the wonderful slideshow God has prepared for you." Collecting
        all those unusual seashells

And some of the ancient sea glass that had been tossed into the ocean
        long ago,

Making the sands and the salt of the ocean create something so beautiful

And natural.

The warm salty breeze blowing against my body,

As if it were being whisked by the softness of an angel's wings.

Seeing the ships in the distance,

Drifting as though they were gently being lifted up,

And back down again as they ride the waves of the far-away view,

As I stand near the water's edge,

And of course I would be thinking to myself of

Where its travels will end.

I love the euphoric feeling of spring

And the smell of a freshly mowed lawn in the summer,

Picnics with all the cool summer foods,

Those warm evenings in the park with a blanket spread on the ground,

Watching the Fourth of July fireworks light up the evening sky.

The laughter of children at play,

Baby puppies,

A warm smile from someone standing in the long checkout lane for that
    last-minute shopping on Christmas Eve,

And everything, and everyone who is familiar to me,

That warm feeling of coming home,

And to know that I have made just one person laugh out loud for a few
    seconds out of each day of my life.

My list of inspirations could go on and on,

For I have learned to remove faulty perceptions

And see things as they really are.

For my bubble was burst

When I no longer was disillusioned into believing that Santa Claus was
the true giver of all free gifts,

But when we learned the magic of giving of our own true selves.

THIS ONCE UPON A LIFETIME OF MINE

With a whisper of a breeze that blows against my bare flesh, I feel the
sudden urge to climb to the top of the highest mountain, and
shout with a stentorian (loud) voice, "Oh, how happy I am to be
among the living." But it is only for a short span of time that I
feel this desire within me. Soon it will vault from my soul as
an unwelcome guest in my body. The breath of life will soon
expel itself from this barren flesh that cries with a perpetual rack
that can never be filled, always wanting, craving the unknown
knowledge that it does not even discern is there.

I cry for all the loves that have passed my way in this life, never giving
homage to reach out to me, to touch the tips of my heartstrings,
leaving them to dangle without emotion.

I cry for all the days that I wasted upon some foolish goals that were
but a dim, brisk light that entered only for a second into the
crowded, eternal horizon of my mind. There was a time when my
intentions were dedicated to the utmost, to discern the feelings
that crept deep within, to search out these plans that were in this
once upon a lifetime, within this life of mine.

I cry for all those days I have missed, for not taking that long walk in a spring rain. Oh, such beauty and splendor lay there before my blinded eyes, those sparkling days that looked as though they were filled with the rich diamonds of Mother Nature's free gift to me. To see a red bird dipping its small beak into a clear fountain of fresh rain, to taste the pure water, a gentle spring rain that would have cleansed this human temple. Oh, but I let the fear of the loud thunder keep me sheltered from this beauty from heaven.

I cried through all my youth, as though I was a small plant, planted very shallow into the ground. My tears fed this temple of mine, and soon I grew into a much stronger branch of this life. And now, as I find myself approaching the years of the eternal end to this once upon a lifetime of mine, I cry for all that I no longer have. I now find myself left with only grim moments of wasteful wishing, trying to recapture but a single year of this once upon a lifetime of mine, to clear a path for my eternal soul.

Oh, but life does not always agree with one's wishes as it comes to its close. And what do we have left to be reminded of all that has crossed our path in this once upon a lifetime? A mere name, with two dates: one of our expected arrival and another of our unexpected departure, engraved on a slate of cold marble.

I can no longer climb mountains so high, or run like a wild and free deer in a lush, green forest, for these legs are no longer full of youth, but are weak and brittle, like a frail tree waiting to fall without anyone there to hear the final sound it will make as it crashes to the forest floor.

One may ask at my passing, "Why were there so many tears?" but only silence will they now hear, for I cried in silence throughout that once upon a lifetime of mine, and so shall there be perfect silence in my eternal sleep—no more tears left to wipe from my own eyes, no regrets, for there will be no more. For this body that was once filled with remorse will now be only an old house of that which housed my soul. I will not miss the flowers that I once wanted to see, as you who are left will bring them to me. And no more tears will anyone see, as you look for your last time, on this once upon a lifetime of mine.

NOVEL LIVES, IN MY OPINION

In each of our lives we take a certain path, maybe from a string of events that will lead us to this point in life—that place where we feel we belong. But it is only at the end of our journeys that we can tell the complete story of our lives, chapter by chapter.

The book of life has been written for each of us, and we fill each page of that book with each day we live. Unfortunately, not all stories pertaining to our life events are pleasant ones, and each in their own way is unique, and special. But if all books were written and read the same, there would be no need for many authors, only one!

Each individual with their own personal title to their own life story.

We are all our own authors. We live our own books, regardless of when our lives began, or our color, or our creed. We have that one certain thing in common: We were all created beings, created in God's likeness and image. The King of this library of individual novels (you, I, them, us) as a whole; we are free moral agents, making our own decisions as we choose, according to the laws of God and the laws set forth by man, to keep that perfect balance. But we are all influenced by others' stories, their *Novel Lives,* which takes away from our own novel way of life, and our own personal life events.

We, being in the flesh, desire those things that we cannot have. Those things we have in our presence, we tire of easily. Our *things* become old to us much too soon, and then we find ourselves going in search of something new, something different, and not just for the materialistic things we harbor within our confines. We go in search of another, craving to know their souls—that part of them that only God knows. But being made in His likeness and image, we are *little gods,* without the mercy of our Heavenly Father, controlled by the flesh, and not of the Spirit, that breath of life that was breathed into each of us at conception.

Like wild animals, we go in search of our prey. We hunt, we stalk, we close in for that final kill. That kill is not always a physical act, but it may be spiritual. It is the things of this world that we cannot always see with the human eye that can do the most damage and destroy us, putting a large hole in our souls, like cancer eating away at our physical being, until it is in its last stages before we realize there is something not quite right within us. Through many different symptoms we recognize that it is time to seek out a physician, only to hear, "I'm sorry, it's too late; the cancer is

95

in its last stages. You waited too long. If only you came to me sooner." But we didn't know; our body didn't warn us, until it was too late. And then suddenly we realize our lives are in their final chapter, and soon our book of life will be closed.

We are susceptible to the wants and desires of others; daily we die to our self, being drained of our own wishes and goals. Maybe we are taught this tradition at a young age. Thus, in turn, we tend to make others happy, seeking their approval, not exercising our own decisions or that free moral agent part of us in the beginning. We find ourselves dressing for the approval of others, always keeping up with the styles that come out of another's chapter in their own book; their so-called *Novel Lives*.

Everything we do affects others' life novels, and we do this without even realizing it. It's only when our own books to our personal lives have come to their final chapter that we can see the whole story. And not all stories have a happy ending, because we sometimes write ourselves into a story that we can't write ourselves out of. If we could, every life's novel would end with a happy sigh, instead of a tear. Even shedding tears at the loss of a loved one is somewhat a selfish act, along with a lot of grief, and sadness. For that person knows nothing of their own death, but those of us who remain here to mourn their loss know the ending of their life story. That soul no longer exists in that book. The (body), the breath of life, the (character), the breath of life, is no longer needed.

So when it's all said and done, whose life story was it after all, theirs or ours?

It would be a matter of opinion to each individual, *I* would assume.

NIGHTLY TRAVELS—EXPRESSIONS BY JADE

As the long night starts to unfold her sheets of darkness, I take myself into bed, tired and weary from the day that has now come to its final curtain. Perhaps knowing within my soul all that has occurred this day, the good and the bad, will soon be a part of history.

I stand beside my place of slumber, disrobing, taking off that last garment of clothing that I will no longer need, as my nude body will soon be shrouded beneath the warm covers of my bed.

As my sleepy eyes glance in the direction of the ticking clock on the nearby nightstand, I see the hands of the clock moving so very slowly. My eyes are blinking as I glance with heavy eyelids, seeing behind closing eyes the hands of the clock moving faster. I turn my eyes away from its direction, as if time is playing a cruel trick on me; smiling to myself at the thought of time passing so fast when we do not look upon the timepiece that controls our daily lives.

I quickly turn the fluffy covers back on my clean place of slumber and give my pillows a gentle toss. I slip into bed, taking my position for a transitional trip to a place where time does not exist, not knowing the exact moment my trip will begin, the windows of my soul slowly close. My body is preparing itself for its departure, not remembering what my last thoughts of this day will be, even though my subconscious will hold these thoughts, perhaps for future trips into the unknown places I have yet to travel in my dreams. Knowing where I would like this journey of the night to take me, I not sure that you are going to be there when I arrive, for our journeys into the night will never depart at the same moment. So I wait with great anticipation, as thoughts of you warm my being to the depths of impassioned pleasure.

As I now take that sleeping position on my side, that position that seems as though it is the only correct position in which this tired body can go into its nightly travels, I feel my leg give a jerking movement. The nerves are starting to relax in my body, preparing me for that sweet, silent night, that time in our lives when nothing feels so entirely wonderful, except for the orgasmic times of sweet love and passion. Knowing we will soon be drifting into the future with the timepiece, its hands circle around in that same direction: minute by minute, that instant twinkling of a puny sixty seconds that soon turn into hour after hours, day after days, as do our lives.

I have now arrived at my first destination in my night of endless travel. As I stand in a void, I no longer care to linger in this place where I feel nonexistence, a vacuum of nothingness. I want to travel to that special place where you are, that place where you make my tired body come to life, and open the closed windows to my soul.

I want to be awake this night, not sleeping. I do not wish to share this night with unfamiliar places and faces, for this night is going fast. I can hear the timepiece ticking away, and soon morning will rush in and steal this moment away from us forever; never will I dream this travel again. Hanging onto this time, the hands of the clock move faster now, as I do not look upon its face.

I wish to lay in my bed and dream dreams, perhaps a dream within a dream. I catch a glimpse of you passing in the night. You reach out and take my hand. I follow you to a place where we have never been before in this travel, but will come again I am sure.

I hear the door of the last stage of this nightly travel slam shut as we enter a place where our senses come to life; we can suddenly feel the silence of the night. A slow tune is playing from the music box you gave to me long ago. I am slowly opening the music box; letting the notes float into this place we are, to make it come alive. As I see you start to sway from side to side, I drop the music box and it crashes to the floor, but the notes are circling us, drawing us near. You and this tune, I can see and I can hear.

All at once the light rushes in. "Where is this light coming from?" I ask myself in amazement. Amazed at how the light could come into this place we are in, with no invitation. It intrudes on our moment of closeness, our time of odyssey, our dream within a dream.

My eyes begin to blink as the light engulfs them, and what do I see? The clock on the nearby nightstand, reminding me my nightly travel has come to its end, and again, as in mornings past, I smile to myself and think, "Tonight my trip will begin again."

TO MY HEART I AM NO STRANGER

To my heart I am no stranger,

However, I may be a stranger to you.

My heart will always know me

And to my own heart I must be true.

I cannot tell my heart a lie

And believe within my mind it's true.

I cannot do the things that my heart won't allow me to do.

I cannot love another with only what's in my mind,

For my heart is much more caring

And my mind will fool me

Each and every time.

It is the things we love the most

We keep within our hearts,

But the mind is forever changing,

Like the seasons,

And the tide,

And the heart is forever revealing what it cannot hide.

"To know me is to love me."

I'm sure you've heard this said,

But we must learn to love with all that's in our hearts

And not what's in our head.

Spiritual Poetry

ONE SINGLE CANDLE AND A FLOWER

One single candle,

And a flower in a small vase,

One tear to shed,

As I bow my head in grace,

With my eyes now closed,

I can see His face all aglow.

Was it just because I came to say hello?

It takes so much to please those who are in this lonely world,

But I will continue to settle for those things He has yet to show,

All the treasures I still need to learn and know.

One single candle all aglow,

And that same flower in a small vase,

I can feel His presence,

I can feel His mighty grace,

All because I came to share my heart

And bare my soul.

I made the first step and I will continue to follow.

I no longer wish to be just standing in His shadow.

One small candle,

With its flame getting brighter, and that same flower in that same small
vase,

Has begun to take root.

As I come to share with Him each day,

I can feel more happiness coming my way.

I can now face each dreadful day.

I open my Bible,

And His words seem to rise from its pages.

Something I had forgotten for what now feels like ages.

And it all started with just one small candle all aglow,

And a single flower in a small vase.

This is how I got to know and learn

My correct and rightful place in this world of woe and sorrow.

From all of this I shall let burn

An everlasting light in the darkest hour that comes into my life.

Never put out that *candle* in your life.

Always let it continue to burn,

For it is by the fire we are tested.

And the fragrance of that one, single flower,

It represents us in our darkest and loneliest hour.

But, when in doubt,

Look all around you

And see that in just one single hour,

All of God's little blessings come not only in that (*one single candle and a flower*).

YOU ASKED ME TO PRAY FOR YOU

You called me last night,

And asked me to pray for you,

But I got too busy,

Thought I had much more important things to do.

You asked me to pray for you,

And I didn't even take the time to ask you why,

Even though

As I think back,

I didn't hear you cry, but I do remember a loud sigh.

And I do remember

I reassured you

All would be okay,

But I did not do what you asked me,

For I forgot to pray.

Early the next morning,

My telephone did ring,

And I remembered the sad voice coming from the other end.

However,

It was my friend's number.

But the sad voice I heard was not that of my friend.

I felt a pain deep down inside my soul,

For I knew the news I was about to be told.

"I'm sorry,

But I have some bad news,"

Came the voice to my ear,

"But your friend, my mother, is no longer here.

The death angel came sometime during the night,

And took our loved one on a heavenly flight,

Homeward bound.

And I'm sure she has arrived, for last night

Your friend, my mother, died."

"Oh, dear God, no," was all I could say

As the phone fell from my hand,

And I dropped to my knees

And began to pray.

"Oh, dear Father, forgive me,"

Was all I could say,

For the one last favor my dear friend had asked of me

Was to *pray*.

Such a small request

But I thought she was at her best,

And I could put the prayer off

Until I had more rest.

I didn't know, Father. I thought she would have at least one more day,

And that would give me more time to pray.

Then I felt such a peace come over me,

And I heard God's words,

Your friend understands.

You meant well, and your kind heart was in the right place.

"So you see, My child,

He continued to say,

Let this be a lesson.

I waited last night to hear from you,

But I heard from your friend before closing her eyes,

So very faithful,

Honest and true,

For the prayer she prayed last night was not for her,

It was for you.

OH, WHERE WOULD WE BE WITHOUT PRAYER?

Oh, where would we be without prayer, Lord,

Where would we be without prayer?

Knowing that you care, Lord, where would we be without prayer?

A mother prays for her son in jail.

Where would we be without prayer?

A sister prays for a brother that's ill.

Oh, where would we be without prayer?

A small child seen kneeling beside their bed before they go to sleep

Prays for their pet,

And in silence their prayer is kept,

And it touches the heart of the throne.

Oh, where would we be without prayer, Lord?

Where would we be without prayer?

I care enough to pray, Lord,

And I sincerely thank You, Lord, for the opportunity.

For in my heart, Lord,

I seek my answers from Thee.

Oh, how I need to pray, Lord.

Where would I be without prayer?

RIVER OF DESPAIR

Only God knows what lies ahead, for we have no promise of tomorrow,

As His Word has said.

Life to me at times was like falling into a river with a strong current:

You try and swim against it,

Only to get nowhere;

Always reaching out,

Grabbing for something to pull yourself out. After a while, you get tired,
        so you give up

And let the current of the river take you where it will.

Sometimes you make it,

Sometimes you don't.

Lord,

You were there,

Waiting to pull me from that (*river of despair*)

Even though, Lord,

There were times I didn't think You heard me through my prayers,

When I called out to You,

I didn't think You were there.

But You reached out to me, Lord,

And came into my life.

You gave me strength when I felt so alone

And so scared,

So afraid to go on living, for fear of what lay ahead. You, Lord,

Gave me a reason to want to go on.

For someone once said,

"Expect a miracle today.

Something good is going to happen to you."

Lord, You showed concern

When I thought no one cared.

You gave me a shoulder to lean on

And cry on,

When I felt so full of anger

And heartache.

Lord, You gave me something to look forward to each day,

By the promise of Your Word,

And the promise of Your return.

So, Lord, when I sum it all up,

You gave me the greatest gift I could ever receive:

You gave me salvation

And eternal life.

Thank You, Lord, for reaching out Your hand to me

And pulling me out of that river.

For without Your love,

I would have been lost forever.

DEAR HEAVENLY FATHER, IT'S ME AGAIN

Dear Heavenly Father:

It's me, again!

And at this late hour I have come to talk to my best friend,

And I hope I haven't come too late.

I realize You have much to do,

But You know how my life has been more than any other,

For You, my Heavenly Father,

I know You are my very best friend.

I find that lately,

More than times past,

I can't seem to be the kindest or friendliest,

I do and say things to others at times,

That I know are so very wrong,

And I cry when I am alone,

For my intentions are never

Ever meant to do this.

I know what I am doing is wrong,

Because I can feel You there in my heart,

Reminding me so very strongly all the time,

And I know my conscience has not been seared like that of a hot iron.

Yes, Heavenly Father,

You have taught me very well

What I am to do.

All the right that is seen in me by others

Is Your light shining through.

But, oh Father, I don't know how to control this anger that seems to
always break through inside of me,

Except to come and talk with You;

And this is for sure not the way I would like to be,

But what You would have me do.

I can't just open up and share all these feelings with anyone.

And this is the reason You sent your precious Son,

A man who had feelings like me,

But could control them,

And offered His fruits for others to see.

I am constantly calling out to Him each and every day,

And I do this mostly when I pray.

I write to Him my prayers,

As I am writing to You right now.

I know that You are Him,

And I know that He is You,

For I have read in Your Word

All the wonderful things You do.

Why, Father,

Am I the way that I am?

I have to sincerely apologize,

But I just don't understand, for when I go to do good,

I find evil is always there,

Or I can count on him to be waiting and lurking somewhere.

I just wanna be the person you, Father, intended for me to be,

Not someone mean and nasty all the time.

I can't handle this, Father,

For the sorrow of it all bears strongly in my soul

And on my mind.

Please set me free,

And bring me closer in my walk in this life

And in Thee.

Please, Father,

This burden gets mighty heavy at times.

And, again, I do apologize for complaining and feeling I have to whine

Like a spoiled brat of a child.

But make me more gentle

And my temperance mild.

I will go now, Father,

But please keep me in mind.

And I'm so very sorry for taking up Your time

With such trivial matters,

These such as mine.

I know the hour is late,

And You have much work to do,

For the harvest is great,

And the laborers are few,

And listening to others,

When they as well come to have a little talk with you.

Amen!

STANDING IN THE DOORWAY OF TODAY

As I pursue my future that remains,

I see many clouds,

But thus far, no rain.

However, I must admit

It would have been so much easier for me

To just give up and quit.

But some way, somehow,

I got through all those crazy times,

And that is when, in my own backyard,

I see the sun begin to shine.

So if I'm on the bottom now, I try my best to look toward the top of all
      things.

Oh, please don't envision that this was how it always was,

For it has taken me a while to finally rise above,

And it didn't happen overnight.

I didn't awaken with a heart filled with love.

It was all that inward anger I carried around inside of me

That kept me blinded;

I could not see.

I didn't understand what was going on,

For there was many a night I stayed on my knees before God

For so very long.

The weight I was carrying was much heavier than I thought,

And I started to forget all the godly things I was taught.

It kept me bound,

Steadfast to the ground;

I could not rise above,

Due to all the anger.

It was taking all my love.

All of those bittersweet emotions

I kept deep inside of me

Only helped my hindsight to become twenty-twenty.

And then one day,

It came with a prayer,

A little reminder someone had sent to me

From somewhere.

I heard sweet Jesus whisper to me,

"Did you forget, my child,

What was taught to you?

I'll carry all your burdens,

Your woes.

I'll give you your heart's desires,

And I'll wipe all the tears from your eyes.

But first you must come to me.

I've been here all the time.

Don't allow Satan to destroy all that was taught to you.

Instead, let Me, your Savior,

Do what I must do."

All I used to dwell on

Was my pain from the past, and now I had been reminded who made me
suffer so,

And in my heart,

I knew I had to let it go.

After that precious prayer,

I knew I was free at last.

When I recall the times

I stood in the doorway of tomorrow,

All I can remember

Is the pain, heartache, and sorrow.

There was no room inside of me

To feel the pleasures of this life,

But now I let nothing stand in my way.

I'm no longer standing in the doorway of tomorrow,

But in the doorway of today.

THANKS FOR THE BOUNTY

I was sitting in this small country diner,

Just outside this town I was passing through,

A very quaint little diner,

Where the seating held very few.

As I was sipping on my hot cup of coffee,

I noticed an elderly gentleman sitting at a small table next to me,

Sitting there alone,

With his hands folded, waiting patiently.

Soon the waitress brought him his order:

A cup of hot tea

And a slice of overly brown toast.

He looked up at the waitress,

And with a warm smile on his face he thanked her.

I could not help myself,

But his manner attracted me

As he bowed his head

And started to say grace.

He closed his eyes

And brought his hands folded closer up to his face.

But that small cup of tea

And that warm toast

Didn't seem like much to me

To bless as his bounty.

And I could not control the tears that started to fill my eyes

As I sat there

And listened with such heartfelt surprise,

As the elderly gentleman kept closed his eyes

And continued to pray,

Giving God thanks for His bounty:

"Dear Heavenly Father,

I ask You to bless this food that I am about to receive for the
nourishment of my body,

And my daily needs,

For this bread I break unto Thee.

And as I sip on my warm cup of tea,

I can't help but pray for all those,

Somewhere out there,

Who will be having much less than me.

"I ask You, Father, to bless the hands of those that prepared this mighty
bounty,

For You see, precious Father in heaven,

In my years, I have come to fully understand

It is not the quality,

Nor in this case,

The quantity,

But for You, Father, allowing me this time to give thanks for your
heavenly bounty."

By this time the elderly gentleman slowly lifted up his cup of almost cold
tea

123

And looked around the small diner,

And his bright eyes stopped when they got to me,

For I guess he could not help but see

What the pure and honest words of his blessing did to me.

I never felt so blessed,

As if he had asked that special blessing especially for me.

And so I felt the need deep down inside to thank Him for this gracious
    deed.

"Thank you, sir.

That was such a precious thing for you to do."

And he answered,

"I didn't only bless this small bounty for me,

But I blessed it for you."

BABES IN CHRIST

It was a long time ago,

But the memories of that small church,

Where we gathered to worship

And cleanse our souls, does not seem to fade

As I grow old.

I was but a child, twelve years old,

And the things of God

I surely didn't know.

Until one day this lady came to my folks,

And off to that church we did go.

Not my folks,

No, they did not take part,

But this elderly lady

Knew, even though I was a child,

I had Christ in my heart.

I looked forward to each and every Sunday

And the prayer meetings during the week.

And so, as time went by, I was called to the altar to bare my sins before
      God,

And to accept Him as my personal Savior,

And the Holy Spirit I wanted to seek.

Oh, the milk of God's words tasted sweet,

And as I grew, I soon was given meat:

Those deep things of God

And the Holy Spirit I did meet.

And then came the day I was baptized in a small country creek,

And my faith only grew stronger,

And I continued to grow in God's Word,

And the Holy Spirit did continue to teach

All those things that some would refer to as being deep.

When we are babes in Christ,

We only receive milk,

But as we continue to grow in His Word, we are given meat,

And I learned over the years that followed,

The faith that can't be tested,

Can't be trusted.

A KIND WORD

In our hearts we know when we do wrong,

And even though it is all due to the *evil one*, we have to take the blame.

But life,

And God's Word has taught me,

A kind word turns away wrath,

And puts the *evil one* to shame.

I thank my Heavenly Father for giving me this mighty grace,

To have the courage, through prayer, to look the *evil one* in the face,

And to stand my ground for the kind things that may come my way,

Such as blessings

The *evil one* will try to take away.

Even the *evil one* fears the good,

And if we don't give in,

The *evil one* will run away.

So even though it may take every ounce of strength you have,

And it may hurt at times,

In the end

We will have clean hearts

And a clearer mind,

Not filled with *evil*,

But much love instead.

Again, I remind you,

No matter how tempted we may become,

For God's mercy and His mighty sake, don't give in to that temptation.

Don't let him think he has won,

For this only gives more power to the *evil one*.

AN ANGEL IN THE MAKING

Friendship that is built on a lie, in time will surely die.

But a friendship where the truth is spoken will not easily be broken.

(For my poetic friend (Eva-FreeSpirit)

Bonjour, my poetic friend!

It is so very warm and wonderful,

To come and visit with you once again,

Even though it may not be face to face,

We have managed through this new age

To feed one another with hope, peace,

And grace.

Miles cannot keep apart what two friends feel in each other's heart.

I must say I love this humble poem you have placed here on your site,

To be shared by you with others,

With much delight.

What a humble write.

In God's eyes, you are one of His brightest stars,

And the *movies* you may not star in

Is not the script God handed for you to play,

But you are precious and unique,

In your own God-given way.

A friend to many,

And a star to all,

An (*angel in the making*),

That's who you are.

So keep smiling, my free-spirit friend,

For one day soon, our own burdens we'll no longer have to bear.

But for as long as you are here on God's earth, I,

Your online poetic friend will always care,

And be right here to share,

And I will always carry a prayer in my heart,

And thank God for friends like you.

So for today,

This moment,

For me and when you dream,

Dream of heavenly things,

For I am just a prayer away,

No matter how far the distance.

And maybe, if it be God's Will,

I will meet you face to face one day,

And until that time arrives,

May God always bless that

Free spirit within you, that will never die.

(For Eva-FreeSpirit by her poetic friend Jade on 06/28/04)

AN ANSWER TO DONNIE'S LETTER

Dear Donnie:

I write this letter with an answer to the question you posed to me.

And in answering this *question*, I will be as open and as honest as I can
be.

It is not what we have on the outside,

But what God places within,

And we are all placed where Christ has already been.

We cannot judge ourselves with the carnal mind,

For if we do, no peace shall we ever find,

But only with what God has placed within,

And that would be the Holy Spirit until the very end.

Just maybe, God positions each of us in a certain place

At a certain time,

And there we must sometimes wait,

For He is never in a hurry,

But He is never too late.

To take the hand of one who may be lost,

And through the kindness of our Spirit-filled hearts,

We lead them from the darkness into the light,

And lead them as well to the cross.

We must always be humble

And sometimes follow behind,

Follow that chosen one that was sent

To lead us into God's divine presence.

And there we will forever be in God's grace,

But we must learn to follow with only our faith.

So you see, my dear poetic friend,

It's not where we're going,

Nor is it where we've been,

But it is where we meet in the final end.

A face is not important,

Nor the words we may sometimes read,

But the empathy for a lost soul

That pleads to be set free.

So I will close this letter, my dear brother in Christ,

With the same kind of love and compassion

God has given me.

KIND WORDS FROM A STRANGER

"Good morning,"

Came a voice, as I turned to see who this was speaking to me.

And as I looked,

I thought to myself, *Who could this be?*

For I did not know this stranger,

But he was kind in his manner as he continued to stare at me.

"Excuse me, sir,

Do I know you?" I had to ask.

And the stranger replied,

"Does it really matter if you know me,

When I just say 'Hi,'

Or 'Good morning' to you?"

"I never really thought about it in a manner such as yours,

But thank you, sir.

That was nice of you,

And this same thing I shall remember to do."

I turned to walk away,

And then suddenly, I realized who this stranger could be.

This one with a smile, especially for me.

For one never knows.

For this I had forgotten, until that one morning came a voice with a kind
and warm stare.

Hebrews 13:2: *Be not forgetful to entertain strangers,*

For thereby, some have entertained angels unaware.

REMEMBERING

As we go through this life,

We learn that it is the *remembering* of others,

For in our Heavenly Father's eyes,

We are all brothers and sisters.

We are His creation,

And we learn a great lesson in dedication.

Birthing must come,

And then after every birth, life has begun.

When we are young,

We can't wait to grow older.

But in between the fleeing years

That suddenly disappear,

We find ourselves asking,

Where did all of my youth go?

We all had to crawl before we could walk,

And we all were silent

Before we learned how to talk.

Some of us were taught at an early age,

Be careful of the words you speak,

For when we are angry,

Malice tastes sweet.

But after these bitter words have been set free

And spill from our lips,

Like sipping on a cup of unsweetened tea,

And you have expressed yourself,

You'll find at one time or another,

Those words spoken in anger you will have to eat.

So as we make our way

Through each and every day,

Make someone smile,

It won't hurt a bit.

Always try to make it a good habit,

And try hard never to quit.

Remembering you are the one who is special,

As long as you make life sweet,

And then when you are old,

Those malicious words that were spoken in anger all through your youth,

You won't have to eat.

HEAVEN'S SPLENDID SYMPHONY

My hand fumbles for the doorknob,

Eagerly anticipating what this glorious new day would have waiting for
me,

As I would walk out into this new morning, pointing my nose in an
upwardly direction,

Taking into my nostrils the smell of a freshly mowed lawn,

That certain smell that reminds me of summer in all its perfect splendor.

That inviting smell of the newness of a summer's morning,

So inviting as I breathe in a deep breath

And release it with a sigh.

As I take my first step into this new day, I feel a gentle breeze brushing
across my face, as a strand of my hair tickles the cheek of my
face.

Quickly pushing my hair behind my ear,

I feel the gentle breeze of this midsummer's morning,

Like the softness of God's breath whispering to me,

As in special moments past,

Once again reminding me, "I am here beside you,

And it is our private time.

Come and let Me show you a marvelous wonder."

I hear the morning doves,

As they sing a special tune written for my ears only.

I stand in the now silence of their lovely song,

My ears finely tuned,

Seeing with my ears,

What my eyes cannot see: heaven's splendid symphony.

A symphony my guardian angel has arranged for me on this special day.

I feel my guardian angel take my hand,

Like the melody I feel deep within me,

With the gentleness of the purest kind of heaven-sent love.

I am being led to a lovely flowering meadow,

Lying on my back with my face pointing upward toward the sky.

I feel the warm, cozy blankets of clouds covering me with such
　　　　tenderness.

"Could this be the wing of doves shrouding me?"

As my guardian angel lies there next to my perfectly relaxed body,

Whispering in heaven's splendid symphony,

Angels singing,

Think with your heart, child,

And not with your mind,

For the heart is much softer,

So very kind.

Use your heart, child, when you look at all things.

No sight is needed,

For when we think with our minds,

Instead of our hearts,

We see things in a different light.

The mind can be misleading,

But the heart is always true.

So think with your heart, child,

It will never deceive you,

For heaven's splendid symphony comes in circles of time,

But this can only happen, child,

When you think with your mind.

So keep this thought inside,

And never let it part,

For heaven's splendid symphony comes only in your heart.

My guardian angel gently brushed the tears from my now-weeping heart,
     for the words of this heavenly song went deep into my soul.

And as she guided my blind eyes to see the gates of heaven unfold,

The orchestra began to play in perfect harmony,

This music we can only hear with our hearts,

Heaven's splendid symphony.

YOU WERE THERE

You saw me through all the tribulations I've been through,

And without You, Heavenly Father, I would not have known what to do.

(*You were there*), Father,

You spared me from the hands of this earthly system,

And the hands of evil men.

I had no place to turn,

And You showed me the door to walk through,

And I opened it,

And You called me to You.

I came out *bag and baggage*, with no place to go.

These were just the words I heard when they called my name,

For I had nothing, Father,

But Your promises to claim.

I stepped out, Father,

And on my faith I came,

And it was You that I embraced,

And it was Your words I proclaimed.

Oh, Father, those years I spent in the valley were long,

But not one time, Father, did You forsake me,

Or leave me alone.

(*You were there*), Father,

And I made it thus far,

And for all the wrong I have done,

You forgave me,

And my burdens you did carry.

So I stand for what you made me.

I am known by my fruits

For others to see.

Even though I walked through that fiery furnace,

And the flames of Hell

I did feel,

I came out with victory,

And my body was not singed,

For (*You were there*), Father,

And will be unto the very end.

ANGEL FRIENDS

I look at each day as a new adventure, a new day to search out the new

And remember that which is old.

For all of it will forever be a part of me.

To meet new friends,

And all the fun it is to get to know them,

To have someone you know will always be there,

No matter the distance

In your heart and theirs, you know you care.

Now, they may be just passing ships,

Passing in the night,

And once we see them, we never look back.

Oh, but there are those who we'll never forget,

For we were on that same ship that passed in the night.

We make each other laugh,

We make each other smile,

And even make each other cry,

But the tears come only because we care,

And wishing all the time when they are in great need,

We could always be there.

Just to hold them and let them know we are real,

Not just words typed on a screen,

But so we can show them our true emotions,

Let them be seen.

We tell each other things we could never share with anyone else,

And hold each and every word we share deep inside,

Where we really care.

So you see,

It's not who we are,

Or even who we would wanna be,

It's all that love

We found to be truly free,

More than a family,

But our own special angels

That live only in our hearts.

I try and imagine all the things I don't really know about them,

But those little matters mean nothing, simply because they are my own
private angel friends.

HIS PICTURE

I couldn't tell you what He looks like,

For my eyes have not yet seen,

Only pictures in my Bible,

And perhaps a picture or two in my dreams.

But there are pictures of the King of Kings

In so many unknown places

And in so many homes.

In my heart, I feel what these eyes have not yet seen,

For I know

By and through my faith alone,

He is my Lord and Savior,

And the holy and mighty King of Kings.

HE HAS RISEN

Welcome back, Lord!

I knew You wouldn't be gone long,

For You only went for a little time to create for each of us that special
heavenly home.

And when you left, Lord, for that short time,

You did not leave us alone,

For the Holy Spirit was here with us all the time.

Our teacher of things,

And to each of us who ask,

He always brings.

Well, Lord,

They say it's Easter Sunday today,

And we all know what that symbolizes.

For you, Lord, have returned.

Glory be to the heavenly host,

The King of Kings,

And this, Father, I surely know what it means.

No, Lord,

I didn't dress up in fancy attire today

And go to church

To worship this reminder of Your return.

But I did remember You, Lord,

And what I remembered the most, Lord,

Was how You had gone away

That dreadful day at Calvary,

When our Savior was nailed to the cross and crucified.

But I do understand, Lord,

It was a part of God's holy plan.

And when You came out of that tomb,

You came out as a man,

As You did when You went in

To be the bearer of all who sin.

So, Lord,

I say to You,

As You have said to Your children,

"He has risen." We love You, Lord,

And thank You for all You have given.

Amen!

WHAT DO YOU SEE?

Can you feel her pain?

What does it remind you of?

Maybe someone she loved had been taken from her.

Can you feel her pain?

Does your empathy have its own way to explain?

When I look at her on her knees,

And looking up toward the heavens,

I can feel her crying out,

Oh God, why me?

Why must I suffer this agony?

I can't stand this pain deep down inside of me.

Oh God, help me to deal with this, if You please.

What do you see when you look at the expression/s on her face?

I see pain,

Like no other could ever erase.

Pain that will not go away,

But will forever remain,

And only time will mend what she is hiding inside.

I can see the agony of defeat.

She has been broken down,

To the limit. She cannot feel her own heartbeat.

What do you see when you look at many others who suffer in many
        ways?

The torment of life will not make a human strong or brave,

It will only help them to an early grave.

Pain, heartaches, and sorrows,

Grief of there being no tomorrows.

So when you see her or him,

Know we all have to hurt sometimes,

And during that time, you just want the world to go away,

And never come again another day.

ANOINTING HANDS

Did you know that Jesus had anointed hands, and whom He touched, He healed.
It was the anointing God, His Father, gave Him to do His Father's will.

Jesus was in His thirties when His first miracle he did perform.

When He turned the water into wine for a wedding feast,

And from there He continued on.

Many followed after Him to see His miracles performed.

He touched and healed the oldest

As well as the newly born.

Anointed hands exist to this very day.

When someone has the gift of healing as they touch you,

They pray,

To lay their hands upon you,

And seek a petition,

Giving thanks before seeing, because it is their faith in God that actually
does the healing.

Anointed hands are praying hands, as they touch you tenderly

And go before the throne with such a healing plea.

We may not recognize these miracles as on each they are performed.

In each individual they may differ from time to time,

But where all healings must begin is within each individual's mind.

A renewing of the Spirit must first be transcribed

To heal from within, before we're healed outside.

ANGEL GIRL

It was a cold, dark night. I had gone for a long walk, was feeling weary

And all alone,

For my lover and I had just had a very bad fight.

I followed the sidewalk down to the end of the city block,

And there on the old courthouse, I looked to see the time on the old
        courthouse clock.

Noticed it was getting late and much colder as the wind picked up,

And the snow started to blow.

I had not dressed for what was about to come,

So I picked up my pace

And started to run,

Saying a silent prayer for help,

And praying to God to send me someone.

All at once I felt as though I was floating on a soft, gentle cloud,

Being kept warm by the softness of an angel's shroud.

My eyes I kept closed for fear of what I might see if I opened them.

Who or what would be carrying me?

I must be dreaming,

I kept repeating under my breath. Or was this my own death? "Please
      do not fear," came a gentle,

Sweet voice from out of nowhere,

"For God heard your prayer,

And He sent me here."

All at once I found myself standing alone

At the entrance to my home.

I had no clue as to how or what brought me there.

As I looked through the blinding snow,

There I saw her,

The angel girl, disappearing into thin air.

She had a glow about her that made my view clear,

And I felt her presence as I was left standing there all alone,

On the front porch of my home.

She turned and said for only my ears to hear,

Remember our Lord's last words:

"I will never forsake thee,

Or leave you in your darkest hour."

I felt the warm tears dripping down my cheeks,

For the words I last remembered from the angel girl left me silent and
      without speech.

JUST ONE MORE MILE WITH JESUS

From the time I could first remember,

I knew I had a chosen path

That I had to follow,

And at the time,

I didn't give it much thought as to which direction I would have to go.
But soon I grew into a young lady,

And this was when I knew,

(*Just one more mile with Jesus*) was the journey I grew to trust and
know.

As I followed throughout God's marvelous land,

I grew tired at times and He would reach for my hand.

"Come, My child,

Hold onto Me. (*Just one more mile with Jesus*),"

He would remind me.

I always felt safe

With my hand in His,

And I knew where He was leading me,

(*Just one more mile with Jesus*) meant in heaven I would soon be.

I never one time gave any thought to how far (*just one more mile with
Jesus*) would be,

Because all through my walk with Him,

I had my reward with me.

HOW THE WEST WAS WON = (ONE)

As far as the east is from the west, so far has He removed our
transgressions from us.

Psalms 107:12–14

If one is looking to the east,

And continues to go in that eastwardly direction,

It reminds me of when the Lord says how far our sins are cast,

As far as the east is from the west,

And they are to be remembered no more.

And the only time

We see the west whence our sins were cast,

Is when we continue to look back.

So continue to tarry eastward, my dear ones,

And remember these words of the Blessed Son.

Keep trotting eastward,

Leaving all your sins behind,

It's never too late,

There is always that permitted time

To make that journey with our crosses to bear,

Knowing God, the Heavenly Father, will always meet us there.

Our journey through sin carries us many a mile,

But when we walk in grace,

We will find at the end of our journey,

It was all worthwhile.

For when we come to the end

Of where the west was (*one*),

There's where we meet the Heavenly Son.

Because we never looked back where we came from,

His light continued to guide our path,

And in so doing,

Destroyed our fleshly wrath.

And like a Father pitied His children,

And as He also says,

He knows our frame. He remembered that we are dust.

So one last thing I must say before I close,

My brothers and sisters in the Lord,

Lay that sickle down,

And get in line,

For our Heavenly Father is never in a hurry,

But He will always be right on time.

And to You, Father, I know I was found,

When I thought I was lost,

And You did toss all my sins away,

Never to be remembered by me from day to day,

And for this I did pray,

In Jesus' precious name.

Amen!

LESS, OR A LOT, BUT NEVER ASK WHY

I stood alone one day at the ocean's shore. I had no one at my side.

I just wanted to be alone

And do a bit of soul searching. And I realized

My soul felt empty and dull inside.

I must have just stood there staring as far as my eyes could see.

No ships could be seen.

I didn't even feel like a living human being.

I turned and walked slowly,

Letting the warm saltwater wash across my bare feet.

I had no place special I had to be,

So there I was,

Just God and me.

And then it finally occurred to me:

I really hated the feeling of memories,

Bittersweet; not something that was easy for me to eat

Or swallow.

They all felt the same,

Nothing but hurt and pain.

Even what some would refer to as happy moments in time

I had nothing to recall but sadness,

Even my own happy memories

I did reframe.

"Why, God, do I feel this way inside?" I silently prayed.

I continued to talk to God as I slowly strolled along,

Alone.

I asked Him, *Why did even my happy moments in life feel sad to me*

When they would come into my memory?

I missed all the good things I once had,

And what should have remained happy memories of old friends,

And lovers,

And even of my own dad.

I suddenly spoke aloud,

"I want it all back.

I want light in my life,

And all these eyes of mine see when I think back

Is the grief

And the color black.

I do not wish to be the way I am,

And feel what I carry inside."

All I could hear was the roar of the ocean answering me.

I guess God must have been too busy.

However, I know our time is not His,

And maybe soon, He will make everything right so I can at least live.

So I turned

And walked away

And thanked Him for His time that day.

And I know as time goes by,

He will wipe the tears from my heart

And eyes,

And I shall never ask Him, *Why?*

For I am starting to feel

Everything is gonna be all right.

And even if I think it's not,

I'm gonna be thankful from now on

For what I've got,

Less or a lot.

And I'm so thankful for God

Just allowing us this chance to talk.

THE LOSS OF A CHILD

I can say this

And be honest:

I know the feeling of losing a loved one.

But the feeling of losing a child,

I can't even imagine the pain inside your hearts.

You bring a child into this world,

And watch them grow,

And even when you're no longer young,

And they are old,

To a mother, they are still a child,

For age does not change what we feel inside.

But when that dreaded time comes,

And they go before us,

We can't understand why.

It's not supposed to be this way.

You think you should have gone first,

And they should have stayed.

And we ask, "Why

Did it end this way?"

Well, we as being human have no clue what God has in store for me and
for you,

But we know *His will shall be done on earth as it is in heaven.*

So on this sad day when you lay your loved one to rest,

Just think now, *He is finally home,*

And in God's rest.

They have been through

What we who are living still have to do,

And, if given a choice, I think they would rather stay right where they
are,

And forever be your guiding star.

Oh, they never leave us,

They are in the gentle breeze that blows,

And you feel the warmth each time the sun shines.

And when you see a lovely rose.

Just think *This is the one whom God has chosen.*

So if you can,

Don't weep for them, for they are in a much better place,

And the vision of your child's handsome face

Will forever remain in your loving embrace.

THIS TIME TOMORROW

Oh, Lord,

I have no idea what has come over me lately.

Could this be a divine test?

And will I pass Your request?

I feel a spiritual battle going on within,

But I know if I endure,

You, Father, will win in the end.

I find when I go to do that which is good,

The evil one comes in and tries to take away all my blessings You have given for this day.

I know the right thing to do.

I should seek Your presence

And pray,

My spirit is willing,

But this flesh is weak.

You know how it is, Father,

For You created me this way.

My heart is heavy laden

And my thoughts are not that of the heavenly kind.

So I pray, Father, for that peace within my heart,

Soul, and mind.

Help me to accept that which I cannot change,

And to be more patient.

And do not put me, Father, too far out of Your range.

For it is times like these

That I so long to please,

As I kneel to pray each day.

I believe,

And my faith has carried me thus far,

And I know, Father,

I shall be seeking Your grace again (*this time tomorrow*).

Thank You, Father, for being there for me once again,

As in many times since passed,

And we both know

This shall not be our last.

So for now, Father, I shall be on my way,

And once again, thank You, Father, for listening while I pray.

And most of all,

For giving me just one more day.

Amen!

TODAY

Have you even given thought to what God put into just one single day for
      each of His children to see,

Each in their unique and own special way?

No one sees each day the same,

For it is our own individual gift from God for us to claim.

But when I open my eyes each new God-given day,

I know I am more than just blessed, for I am so very thankful that I can
      show how much I can truly care,

And appreciate what God has freely given unto me to share.

I, as well as many, have my private moments of meditation and
      inspiration

And prayer,

Where I go to bare all my burdens, and I know He will meet me there.

Oh, yes,

He talks to me in that so-gentle voice,

As if it were a warm, gentle breeze;

But only when He is invited in,

For my Heavenly Father is a perfect gentleman.

I bow my head,

And get on my knees to pray.

I get to have a little talk with my best friend,

And not one word does He not hear.

I can bare my complete soul

Without doubt or fear.

I then hold onto that blessed hope

And my Father's promises to me,

For I know what I have asked him in private,

He will reward me openly.

Oh, thank You, Father, for this moment you have allowed me to spend
with you (*today*),

And for always listening when I take the time to pray.

And as I continue to travel through this glorious day,

I will not take thought of tomorrow,

For You, Father, will continue to have Your own perfect

And divine way,

Just like You created (*today*).

Ahhhh, yes,

(*today*).

What a small title.

But it has so much to offer,

For in just (*today*),

There will always be just one Author.

Love Poetry

OH, IF ONLY

As I lay sleeping in the still of the afternoon, the warm ocean breeze blows through my bedroom windows, making the sheer, white curtains float on the invisible shroud of the wind bringing you once again into my room. As you suddenly appear at the foot of my bed, my sleepy, shut eyes catch a dim glimpse of you standing before me. Your white long-sleeve shirt unbuttoned, exposing your manhood, as your pants cling low on your hips, no shoes on your feet. Your ghostly image hovers just above the wooden floor; you look down at my sleeping body, and I feel your blood boiling through your veins, your eyes glowing with a beam of light that burns deep within my soul, transmitting the passion from your being into mine, causing my sleeping body to stir in my bed, wanting you, desiring your touch once more as if it were just yesterday when we touched for the very first time. The first time, when our love was but a burning flame, that flame now torturing me as I am craving your touch, but you beckon my love from a distance now. Please come and quench this raging fire that burns deep within my soul, craving you.

(Oh, if only) you could come and share this empty space inside my aching heart, and fill this empty space beside me here on our once-bed of love.

(Oh, if only) you could come and place moist, wet kisses upon my cold lips that have hungered for your warm breath.

(Oh, if only) you could come and make love to me just one more time, and let me feel once again what I have missed so. I now sleep only to bring you back into my life, calling you from that world of silence that keeps you from me now.

(Oh, if only) I could go back to that first moment in time when we were together, to savor what I took for granted at that moment, seeing your warm eyes smiling into mine as we reached peaks of passion that filled us to the top. Our cup runneth over with pleasure for one another.

(Oh, if only) I could have captured that moment, never giving a thought that you would have to leave me one day. I now lay in this dream state, waiting for you to return to me as though we were meeting for the first time.

(Oh, if only) you were not so familiar to me. Perhaps if you were but a stranger in the night, only passing through my dreams, you would not linger, making me grieve for you so, the tears running down my cheeks and puddling on my pillow.

(Oh, if only) I could awaken from this sleep to find I was only dreaming after all, and you lay nestled next to me.

(Oh, if only) I could stay in this place where we meet now, never to awaken to an empty longing that haunts my waking hours.

(Oh, if only) you did not have to return to a place of no feeling, no remembrance of me, that place I never was. I want to lay with you once again as we did in our youth, not giving any thought to this moment that has suddenly crept upon us as a thief waiting in the night to rob us of our mortality.

(Oh, if only) I could hear you whispering my name in that so-gentle voice that I hear now only with my heart. Wait! I hear you! I hear you in the distance calling me. Help me to answer you.

(Oh, if only) this could be real.

(Oh, if only) you could stay but a while longer. Do you really have to leave me now? I see you drifting on the wind once again to that place I have yet to travel.

(Oh, if only) you could come and visit me again as I sleep, I would but sleep forever.

A ROSE AT THE END

There is a rose that is given to me.

It is always special,

And it will always be.

The rose has no color,

It's only black and white,

No luscious reds,

And it's not even bright.

There is no smell of perfume

To sniff as I raise it to my nose,

But to me it is the most precious rose.

It is the signature of someone I love,

For at the end of each letter, he signs with a rose.

I will treasure these letters for as long as I live,

Reading each one carefully as the petals unfold; not missing a word,

For when I come to the end, I will find the rose.

These letters will live long after I'm gone.

Our children will love them—

Letters from their dad that were sent to their mom.

And on my last day, when I am laid to rest,

I want black and white roses, for they are the best.

I will need no smell to lift to my nose,

For at the end will be the signature of the rose.

WHEN HE SAYS "I LOVE YOU"

We all have our doubts

And are afraid of being hurt by the one who *rocks our world*,

Or maybe being taken for granted,

But it's up to you.

You have to put into it what you get out.

It's a two-way road,

And not left up to just one to carry the load.

It takes two to stay,

But only one to be on their merry way.

So if you can remember these words,

And what they say,

You'll have that kind of love

That will never go away.

When that special someone says, "I love you,"

And you wonder if they do

Each and every time they tell you,

Stop for a moment,

Or maybe even two,

And really examine those three words: *I love you.*

They may not always send you roses,

Or buy you pretty things,

Even a huge diamond ring;

But sometimes it's the little things they do for you

That at the moment go unnoticed,

That mean the most,

That prove that their love is really real.

A gentle kiss upon your lips,

Matching and clasping each other's fingertips,

Your small hand inside of his, that part of yourself and his that you give.

Snuggling on the sofa

On a cold winter's night,

Holding each other so very tight,

Your feet in his lap, as he massages your toes,

As you're both watching the warm fire glow.

The flickering of the candlelight as you look into each other's eyes.

It's at that moment that you feel love grow.

Hold onto it.

Don't let it slip from your grasp,

Like pouring out the wine

From a lovely wine glass.

Sip on it,

Savor its delight.

Always make memories both day and night.

And of all the feelings you sometimes have,

Just try to be happy,

In love, and be glad.

Remember and promise yourself this one special vow: Believe him
when he says *I love you*

Because he's loved you the best he knows how.

STANDING IN YOUR SHADOW

We walk in the silence of another's footsteps. As their shadows are
      casting its light upon us, we turn and find that person is no longer
      there. We find we are standing alone,

No longer standing in the shadows of another's dream,

But in our own dream.

I dream of being in your shadow

As your warmth covers me daily with the shadows of your love and
      kindness.

You share with me from your heart.

You fill that hole in my soul like no other could ever do.

When I have felt like a wounded bird,

You lift my wounded spirit

And make it soar with the eagles.

You reach down

And pick me up

And smooth my ruffled feelings

With only that so very gentle touch you have.

You embrace me

And place a huge kiss on my heart.

I can smile once again at all the pain I have seen for that time,

And feel myself begin to take flight into another day in the shadows of
     your love.

To walk in the shadows of your love and strength

Is like a renewing of all I have missed in this life.

The light you cast on my heart and soul will burn forever.

As long as I know you are there in front of me to lighten my path,

I will forever walk in your shadow,

And follow you to the end of all time.

In your shadow is my safe haven.

TO LOVE YOU WITHOUT A DOUBT

I have,

(*Without a doubt*), grown to love you

And all your little quirks. However, I must admit

I do not always understand them.

I know, (*Without a doubt*), they are what makes you so very special to
    me.

(*Without a doubt*), I am learning to accept what I would never want to
    change about you:

All those little things that may go unnoticed by others,

But have brought you closer to me.

I wouldn't change a thing about you now.

For how can one say, "I love you,

But I wish you were different,

And you would change your ways"?

What brings two together

Should never be changed between them

To tear them apart.

To love you (*Without a doubt*)

Is never having to hesitate for one mote of a second,

To ponder within the depths of my heart and soul

As to the love I have for you, (*Without a doubt*).

Love is not a face,

But a bright light that burns within my heart for you.

I never want to second guess the nature of your being,

For I loved you first without ever seeing you.

I grew to love you from the inside out.

So now I can honestly say

(*I love you without a doubt*).

TO DANCE WITH YOU

Hold me closer than close,

Let me lay my head upon your shoulder

And close my eyes,

As we listen to the sweet music of the band playing our song,

Hold me in your arms all night long.

I never wish for this moment to end,

For I have waited much too long for this time.

Where have you been all my life?

We waited so long for this magic moment to begin.

Hold me in your arms

And cuddle up close,

As though this was always meant to be.

Caress my cheek next to yours.

Whisper in my ear you are in love with me.

Never let me go,

For now I feel the true meaning of love's warm glow,

As we continue to dance to the music,

So close, so soft, so slow.

Morning will not exist in this dream, as we drift across the shining wood
dance floor.

So hold me in your arms all night long,

For I know this is where we both belong.

(*To dance with you*)

Is something I have waited much too long to do.

Everyone is leaving now,

But the band continues to play our favorite song,

Just for me,

Just for you.

We glide across the dance floor,

And make our way outside.

I follow your lead

Onto the balcony,

Where we dance under a million stars

Twinkling in the late evening sky.

For I am your lady,

And you are my one and only guy.

And as I lift my head up from your shoulder

And find your soft lips,

You guide your hands down to my small waist

And place them on my hips.

You bring your hands back up

And place your long fingers within mine.

(*To dance with you*) is my perfect dream that did come true.

And as I wake in my bed

And realize it was only a dream after all,

I glance up

And there I see our silhouettes upon my bedroom wall.

But my dream did come true,

For I did get (*to dance with you*) after all.

A DAY THAT WILL LAST A LONG NIGHT'S TIME

At this moment,

When I find myself feeling totally alone

And empty, I wish I could dream you into my life this night as I sleep.

I would make passionate love to you in ways of the mind. It is but a
dream, this life of ours.

One day of a passing,

A day that will last a long night's time.

I would think in times passing of all we should have had,

But missed,

And it will be during those times I will love you the most.

So, my prince of the evening, I will bid you a good night and, until the
dawn breaks forth,

I shall perish for the touch of your warm moist lips upon mine.

I shall forever seek to look upon your sweet face,

A face,

That one in a million that I seek out among the vanishing crowds before
my eyes looked into yours.

To touch you,

As you know I can only touch you,

For no other can make you so willfully wanting, with such a deep desire
that burns to the core of your being.

I am your master of masters of love.

I come to you in the night, seeking your desire you feed upon,

As I know you wait upon me with greater than great anticipation to
come.

You take me into your warm embrace

And hold me tight with a vice like hunger,

I am but a whimpering child when I am creating, and not just making,
love to you.

That kind and tender love you give to me so freely,

That kind of love that beckons me back from that place you and I know
so well.

So I must tarry into this long night alone,

Searching for you in my dreams,

And that, my love, is life.

A day that will last a long night's time.

AND THE MUSIC PLAYS ON

And the music plays on as the waves of the ocean,

The sun on a hot summer's day, the stars on a clear

Bright night,

In raven with the heavens and the light of the moon.

This heart beats to a different tune,

And the music plays on.

We take our steps one by one onto the dance floor.

I hear our favorite song

As you take me into your warm embrace,

And the music plays on.

Twirling,

Round and round we go,

Not too fast, and not too slow,

Like the silver ball above our heads,

With its scintillant glimmer, like that of sparkling diamonds,

And the music plays on.

I feel the pounding of your heart

With each beat of the drums.

No one is dancing,

Only you and I,

And the music plays on.

We are dancing to a different beat.

Our eyes close

As our lips meet.

I taste your sweet kisses,

More sweet than any fine wine,

And the music plays on.

When will the music stop?

Where will it end?

As the music continues to play in two lovers' hearts

There is no beginning,

There is no end,

And the music plays on.

A SONG OF LOVE JUST FOR YOU

Loving you

I find so easy to do. I want to sing these words of love to you.

I want to hold you in my arms so tight and kiss your sweet lips until the
        morning's light.

I love to love you,

You make it so easy to do.

Where would my life be

If I didn't have you?

A song of love was written for two,

So close your eyes

And I will sing it to you,

As I hold you in my warm embrace

And trace the smile upon your face.

As your eyes are looking deep into mine,

When I am with you there is no time,

For I am yours,

And you are mine.

So hold me close as I hold you.

Let's make this moment last for just us two,

As I sing this song of love to you.

A LOVE LIKE THIS

What is this I write to you this hour? Is it a piece of my heart?

Could it be due to what I am feeling because of the late hour,

And our time we are apart?

I have missed one day too many of your life.

And now in this late hour I am trying to capture a portion of all that
        which I have not had of your life.

I look into our past,

From all the details you have shared,

And I feel saddened.

But my tears were shed many years ago for you.

And I only wish to hear our laughter as though we never shed one lost
        tear between us.

My eyes are no longer sad when I think upon old memories.

But a smile comes to my mind and appears without me knowing it,

And I hear your laughter as well,

As we know this feeling of freedom,

Finally at peace with each other's hearts.

No more shall we be this distant,

And so far removed from that which lives within us now,

A time of caring, a time of love with no boundaries,

A perfect time we have brought back to each other,

And forever this shall remain,

And never again take us apart.

For you are my heart

And I am yours,

And we know our heart cannot beat when separated and dwelling in
each one's body,

But a love of this kind is meant to share.

THE KISS OF DEATH

She sat in the red velvet chair

And looked with a diabolic glare

Out into the heat of the night's burning air.

A place ceased to exist,

For she longed for the taste of her long-ago

Lover's cool, moist kiss.

But now time would not permit her this passionate bliss,

For she was no longer of this place on earth.

She had experienced a rebirth

That tormented her soul,

Both day and night, for fate had come and handed to her

Her unwelcome plight.

From a distance she could admire all those personal things of a woman's
   desire.

No light of a day now existed for her in this torrid place,

Only the darkness could she view in an image of all the pleasure she
   once knew.

Her desires were stronger than she ever could imagine,

For only in the darkness could she view her lover's moist, sodden kiss,

That kiss she so longed to feel as her stomach would ache deep within,

For her lonesome heart ached to be with him.

"Oh, heavens of the light,"

She would cry out,

"Please bring him to me.

Let his journey be swift.

For this one I do desire,

To quench within this burning fire;

To taste of him

What I have longed for

And missed.

Who placed me in the hellish place?"

In the distance, came a slight reply

From the majesty on high,

As she continued to sit there in her red velvet chair

As a queen,

With glaring eyes of green.

And answering in a doubtful

And dubious manner,

She did receive her unwelcome answer,

But the news she was now hearing

Her mind could not accept,

Not even one single word,

For she learned the truth of her dreadful fate.

"You are not whence he now dwells,

For your lustfulness

Has sent your soul to an eternity in hell.

When once upon a long time ago you gave the kiss of death,

You put not one honest man to a silent and peaceful rest.

Those same souls you stole shall roam throughout eternity,

No peace will come to them,

For these souls you stole away

Are now only visible to haunt you night and day.

When once upon their time and yours,

A long time ago,

You gave to each of them the Kiss of Eternal Death,

And to each you kissed,

There shall be no rest.

And again, I remind you,

Those souls you stole

Shall roam for eternity without peace or rest.

In the darkness you now must live.

The price of your own soul,

You, too, as well I did give.

Even though your dry bones in the grave now lay,

No beauty of you there remains.

So now, my sweetness, at last,

The one with all the charm,

As you were well known,

Who has now come here to dwell,

For you found your heaven while on earth.

For now through all eternity,

Your home will be hell."

WHO DOES YOUR HEART BELONG TO?

I remember when we both could relate as to the matters of the heart,

We could not fake.

All felt so right

Between you and I.

There were even moments

When I thought,

If I had wings, I could fly.

I still look at you through eyes of wonder,

With expressions of love that make my heart thunder.

For you are the reasons

I live and breathe,

So how could I ever lose you?

And how could I leave?

So you ask me with a trembling voice,

"Who does your heart belong to?"

And I reply,

"To you, of course."

It is then I hear you sigh.

I kiss your tears

And I wipe your eyes,

And I express,

"Even though we are miles apart,

You and I know who has each other's heart."

Miles do not change what we feel inside,

Nor can it steal

What we sometimes hide,

For I know in my heart very soon we will be

Side by side,

Walking through this life with a graceful stride.

Our hearts will be forever one.

No need for questions,

Only much love,

With so much expression.

YOUR MEMORY

I now stand, staring out as far as my eyes can see,

For there is not a day or an evening your memory eludes me.

It is more than a memory.

It is a time,

Not that long ago,

When in my arms I embraced the shadows of love's warm glow.

Now I stand and look across a distant span of time

And space,

And in a vision, I see your handsome face.

In my heart, I feel a certain pain that cries out to me,

Knowing within,

Nothing can ever remain the same.

I shall wait forever, for this is meant to be,

As I know there can be no existence, no life

Without you, for me.

So hurry back to me, my love, as I stand here and wait

In the same exact place we shared life's fate.

This damnable fate took you away from me, leaving me to mourn your
absence,

But forever anticipating your return.

For if my feet could speak to my heart,

I would turn and run.

But now I know it is much too late,

For my love for you has sealed my fate,

So here I stand, and here I will forever wait.

WHAT HAPPENED TO US?

Yes!

That is the question I ask myself these days:

"What happened to us?" Was it all my fault,

Or was it something that was only to last for a short span of time?

You came into my life like a storm.

Everything was going so fast,

I didn't have time to realize when you started to just drift away

Like the rain on a summer's day.

The showers of your love stopped raining on me,

And now that the storm has finally come

And gone,

I can now see.

I can see only those things I wanted to be,

But time has proven that all of it was wrong for me.

I feel the tears

As they fall on my cheeks,

And they even come when I am asleep,

Because late at night when all is silent in my bed,

I wake with this grief in my heart and thoughts of you inside my head.

Oh, how sweet the taste of love can be in the beginning,

But, oh, how cold and empty a feeling it is when you know that it is
ending.

And you find all that you have left is the memories of that time when two
strangers met,

And, oh God, how hard that part is to forget.

I found an empty spot inside my lonely heart today.

As hard as it is for me to admit,

I know that soon I shall be going away.

For that empty feeling came when I finally realized I could no longer
stay in a relationship where love no longer exists.

I am tired of crying alone

And feeling like I am the only one who cares.

For if life only holds my heart in its hands,

Then I am sorry,

But where does that leave my morals and values of something I can't
understand?

My luggage is now packed,

And sitting beside the door,

As I wait for the final exit from my life and yours.

And a huge part of my heart begs me to stay,

The other part is telling me that I have no choice:

I must be on my way.

I take one last look around the room,

And memories are all I can see and feel

Of a much happier time for you and me.

And I think to myself,

"We should have left well enough alone,

Because a place where love no longer dwells

Can never be a home."

AS I STILL THINK OF YOU,
DO YOU STILL THINK OF ME?

Do you think of me at the oddest times? Does my memory ever cross
    your mind?

What do you recall when your memory drifts back to me?

Do you think mostly of the laughter, or the tears when we had to say
    good-bye?

Do you ever lay awake at night and cry?

Do you get angry with me for what I did to you?

Well, it's okay if you do,

Because I get angry with *me*, too.

But if there could have been a way,

I would have been that person who was so special to you.

Do you ever question yourself,

Why me?

Was I so blinded by the love

I could not see?

No, sweet one,

It was not your fault,

And, God, I'm so sorry I broke your precious heart.

If there could have been some way I could make it all up to you,

If it took the rest of my life, this is what I would do.

I can't be someone

That I never was.

But God knows of all my love I will always have for you.

A warm smile comes to my lips,

And I feel the tears on my heart as they drip

One by one. All the crazy,

Fun things we used to do

Before you met me

And I ever met you.

I will always miss you, forever and a day,

And, oh God, how I wish you could have stayed.

But life goes on,

No matter what,

For the hands on the clock we cannot stop.

If I had only one wish left in my life,

I would wish I could have been your wife.

Fate comes and goes in and out of our lives,

And each time fate arrives,

There is always some crazy, mixed-up surprise

That ends up controlling our lives,

Just some little something that could never be.

So I am left to wonder, *As I still think of you,*

Do you still think of me?

I ALWAYS KNOW WHEN YOU'RE NEAR

I place my hand over my heart, and once again I can feel that same
      sadness that still remains.

It has not left me for a moment since you went away.

I can remember the very first time I looked into your beautiful blue eyes.
      Even though it was dark,

I could see such a glowing spark.

And I know when you are thinking of me,

For I feel you deep within my lonesome, saddened heart.

Missing you has become a part of my life.

I miss you every waking hour

And wish I could once again feel you by my side.

Our lives had to be traveled without the other,

But I can still feel the love we had for one another.

So, my precious darling,

No matter where you are,

I always know when you're near me,

Always and forever so close,

But always so far.

And I will always live with our special memories.

DON'T BREAK MY HEART

How did I get to this place I now find myself in? Did it happen
      suddenly?

Or have I eventually come to realize that it's always been?

The absence of all my emotions,

Always feeling as though I am drifting on a wide-open ocean with each
      wave that rushes in

And takes me back out again.

Don't break my heart,

I've been there one too many times before.

My heart slams shut,

Like the closing of a door.

When I had you inside my head,

You made my blood simmer to a slow boil,

You made me feel alive inside.

No death did come to my eternal soul.

I wanted you forever,

And yes,

And even for one day more,

But you could not return to me what I needed to feel from you.

I could not stop all those crazy feelings you made me feel

And do.

And now I ask you, *Why?*

Was it simply because I openly admitted all the love I was feeling for
you? Please!

I cannot bear the thought of losing you again.

I never wish to return to that state of sadness,

When we are once again apart.

So, please,

I ask you,

(*Don't break my heart*).

YOU AND ME

I saw you today,

But you didn't see me,

For I was hiding beneath the old weeping willow tree,

Its long, finger-like branches completely shrouding me.

I stood there while you were with your new love,

And all I could feel was that same old pain of lost love,

Wishing that it was still me.

I could not hold back the tears as I saw you take her into your warm
          embrace.

I pretended it was my face that you held in your long fingers,

As I watched you placing passionate

Kisses upon her soft lips.

I wanted to be there in her place,

As I continued to stare at your handsome face,

That one in a million to me,

For no other could ever set this heart of mine so totally free.

Yes, I saw you today,

But you didn't see me,

As I stood there beneath that weeping willow tree,

Wishing its long, flowing branches would reach out and hold me.

I could see you walking hand in hand,

And I reached down,

Took both of my hands and held them,

Locked in a tight clasp in front of me.

I had to turn and run away,

For I did not wish to spoil your sweet,

Loving day,

Nor take the chance you might get a glimpse of me.

But just as I started to make my way out of that dream state,

Suddenly, there you were, standing face to face,

Smiling at me.

You looked surprised,

As I suppose you could see the tears in my eyes,

And you asked me what was wrong

As you reached out and took me into your loving arms.

I sobbed so very hard

As you shook me gently,

And told me to awaken from this bad dream I was having.

I tried to hold back the rush of tears,

And you tenderly kissed away all my fears.

I tried to explain to you what I thought I had seen,

But you reassured me,

It was just all a bad dream.

As my heart felt like it would break into,

I realized you still were with me,

And I was still with you.

You took my hand,

And said, "Come,

Let's get out of here,

It's time for us to leave."

And as we walked hand in hand from under that weeping willow tree,

I felt this need to look back.

I saw you,

But I didn't see me.

ANOTHER DAY IN PARADISE

Another day in paradise. This is where I wanna be. This is how I feel
when you are with me.

Another day in paradise takes me away.

When I am with you,

This is where I always wish to stay.

No time exists

When I feel your hot, moist kiss.

Take me on another trip to paradise with you.

Let me feel,

Breathe in the passion just between us two.

I'm never in a hurry when you're so willing to please,

Tease,

And do all those unmentionable things you do to me. Paradise is an
island inside the two of us,

And the pleasure we can create.

Please come for me

As I wait.

A LITTLE LOVING

It doesn't take much,

Just your touch,

And I come alive.

I can't hide all these feelings of love

When I look into your eyes.

(*A little loving*) from you

Makes the skies bluer than blue,

And you make my body start to melt.

Such wonderful feelings

I've never felt.

(*A little loving*) from you

Makes me feel like a free bird

Gliding through space and time

With only you on my mind

So please never stop giving me (*a little loving*),

And promise to never let me go one single day without spending just a
    little time giving back

(*A little loving*) to you too.

FANTASY—YOURS OR MINE?

Come into my fantasy.

Allow me to share it with you,

This place that does not really exist to anyone but me,

This place I find myself always loving to be.

Perhaps there is no other place quite like this I see.

But that's what a *fantasy* is all about,

It's all about the many things

That are special only to me.

It doesn't matter in the least

If it exists or not,

But in each and every fantasy I have,

I can feel them with my heart.

Close out all the world,

And tune into the thoughts within your creative mind,

Knowing that the music you hear

Is the only one of its kind.

And let it take you to that place

No one has ever been,

And feel it deep within,

Knowing if by no other way,

You can only come here if you are invited in,

For it's your world

Made up of all your dreams

Of waterfalls

And swirling, whispering streams,

Which only you can hear.

And, who knows

Once you're there

What else may appear?

In this fantasy of yours,

Close all the windows to your mind,

And lock all the doors,

And allow your soul to come alive

Once you have arrived.

You can run in the open fields,

In the light of the silver moon,

And fall asleep in the golden meadows

Until the late afternoon,

And drift aloft on the floating clouds,

When the day comes to a close,

But only if you so choose.

It doesn't matter who may believe,

If you wish to share

To have this fantasy without heartaches to bear;

Only happy laughter is all you'll find there,

As you may chase lovely butterflies in the mistiness of the air.

And if, by chance, you cannot find your own fantasy,

Then come

And let me take you to mine.

IMPRISONED BY YOUR WORDS

The truth can hurt us more than we may ever really know,

So we keep believing what we are told,

And then suddenly one day,

One week,

One month,

The years pass much too fast.

Then it hits us,

This person you once thought you knew,

Who told you all of this time

They were in love with you,

They lied!

And you had no choice

But to know

The truth,

And you started to feel yourself dying inside.

You cried,

But they never saw your tears.

You hurt,

But they never felt your pain.

You had only yourself to blame,

And all of those poetic feelings of loving

And being loved in return.

You no longer felt inspired,

But pathetic

And petrified,

For death would have been so much more pain free.

And from this pain you were feeling,

You would have been set free.

Now,

You have to mend what has ripped your heart apart.

And when you think how long it will take to forget,

It all goes back to thinking about just giving up,

And dying.

Why was I so blind that I could not see

What I was allowing you to do to me?

But now those times have come and gone,

And I am no longer feeling the pain of going insane.

Yes! Once again I do feel inspired,

And I thank you for all of this knowledge you have made me acquire.

No pain, no gain.

How very true this saying has become to me,

Now that the pain of loving you

Has finally set me free.

I have broken those shackles I was imprisoned in for so very long,

And my heart can rest once again

Because it's back to where it should be.

It no longer belongs to you,

Because now

It belongs only to me.

Never again will it be worn on my sleeve,

And never again will I be a fool to believe

That when we are in love,

We're free,

For when we believe in love we soon become (*imprisoned by words*).

I LIKE YOU

Have you ever had a heartache? Can you relate? That feeling that comes
only after you feel it's too late.

That pain you feel inside your heart, that is a real pain there, when you
feel the one you love no longer cares.

Oh, the misery and the torment. Is it worth all this pain? What does
love bring to us that is such a gain?

I suffered this familiar heartache and this familiar pain,

And here I go once again.

When will I learn

Love is not meant for all?

I thought I wanted it at the time I found it.

Or did it find me?

No matter. Love makes us blind,

For at that time

Love is all we see.

It hurts to be in love.

Oh, all the promises seem to be so right at that time,

Until we turn

And no love is left to find.

And then come the tears with a chest full of pain,

And then we realize we have only ourselves to blame.

And then comes the anger,

And we soon heal,

Just to do it all over again.

But this time,

I will (*like*) you only,

And no matter how lonely I may become,

For when

I feel love on my sleeve,

I will make sure I turn and run,

For (*liking*) you can be more fun.

I LOVE YOU, TOO

(This poem was written for all those who had that once-in a lifetime love
that went away much too soon, but they took that love you had
for them along—and never forget *you loved them too* … True
love never dies.)

I was going through some old things I had packed away,

Thinking when I packed them I would be seeing them again another day.

Well, just as I had planned many years ago,

I found the box of things I packed away, but the strange thing of it all
was

It didn't seem like years ago when I started to open them,

It seemed like only yesterday.

I guess I must have sat there in our room, just picking each item up

And looking at it carefully,

And that time came back to me, when I was a young bride of only
twenty-three.

I used to watch you as you slept each night,

Thinking to myself,

I can't imagine a night without you,

Or a morning waking without you alongside of me.

The way you would always cuddle up close to me,

And hold me tightly as we would both drift off to sleep.

But before going to sleep, there was always something you never forgot
        to tell me,

"Good night,

Sweet dreams,

I love you." And I would always say the same back to you.

Our lives were not always perfect,

We had our ups and downs,

But through it all,

We managed to stick around,

Through the good times and the bad.

We didn't have a lot of money,

And there were times when I didn't think we would make it to the end,

With bills piling up,

And a new family we had begun.

When poverty came in the front door,

Our love didn't go out the back.

We always seemed to pull together,

And soon we would be back on the right track.

We got through those times,

And God gave you and I a lot to be thankful for:

Our precious children,

A little girl

And boy.

But I would give all that up,

Just to feel you snuggle up to me

And hear you say just one more time,

"Good night,

Sweet dreams,

I love you."

And I could say to you just one more time,

"I love you, too."

But that dreaded day had arrived that we both talked about.

Which one of us would God take first?

And you would always say it would be you,

And I would say,

"Well, I hope God takes me then, too."

But things don't always work out the way you wish they would.

One has to stay behind sometimes,

And in this case it happened to be me.

I miss you more than I could ever express, so I sit here and reminisce

Of our youthful days,

And even our first kiss.

And if God would grant me just one wish, this is what I would do:

I would lie in bed all snuggled up close to you,

And hear you say one last time,

"Good night,

Sweet dreams,

I love you,"

And I could tell you one last time,

"*I love you, too.*"

I NEVER KNEW

I wish I could have trusted you,

But you always seemed to make that impossible for me to do.

You always blamed my lack of trust in you on my long-ago, abusive past,

But no,

This was not the case.

For the most part of that long-ago time

Has almost left my crowded mind.

But it was you who taught me the worst part.

You promised to always love me,

And to never break my heart.

But I guess *promises* were made to be broken,

Like you broke my faith

And trust in you,

With the words that were left unsaid.

But until now, (*I never knew*) this person I thought was really you,

And yes, it hurts very much, too.

We had our moments in the beginning,

230

Never giving any thoughts to the ending,

(*I never knew*) until today that you were really this way.

So I had to let you go,

And I had to tell you good-bye.

And yes, I did cry.

But a new day will come on the morrow,

And I will eventually lose all my heartache and sorrow.

I wished you a good life before I told you *good-bye*.

After I was gone,

Did you really cry?

I hope you took my words all in stride,

Because I could not hide what I was feeling inside.

If I only knew

This would have never happened to me, or to you,

For I would have let our beginning also be our ending.

MMMM, TO KISS YOU

I want to kiss your moist, manly lips,

To feel the passion as it grips,

And feel your strong hands on my hips

As you press your body to mine.

There is no other feeling such as this.

Mmmm, the taste of your kiss,

It is one of a kind.

I see you from afar,

And I am waiting

And gazing with this feeling of great anticipation,

As I wait for you waiting for my invitation

To come closer to me,

So as to see.

I can feel your body calling out to me,

And all I can dream of

Is to look and see

You making sweet

Passionate love to me.

I want you to kiss me all over,

And touch me in all those forbidden places,

Forbidden only to others,

But not to you and me,

For we are lovers.

I catch myself calling you with only my mind,

And I turn, and there you stand,

As you reach for my hand from behind.

And there in the crowd, we both stand.

A woman and a man only others may see

But they cannot feel those flames of passion burning inside of you and
me.

We run to take cover from only the others,

In a dark place,

But not dark enough that I can't still see your face

And feel your tight embrace.

I whisper in your ear,

Make love to me,

Take me now.

You push me against the wall of a building, and you moan for what you
will soon be giving,

And I do the same, as I can't think of anything else.

Mmmm, I can smell your manly scent,

And all the hours of making love with each other I know and feel

Will be well spent

In a vortex of provocative sex.

All at once I snap back to reality, as I look at where I thought I saw you
standing,

And I sigh,

And then all the tears come rushing in.

I wanna go back to where we had been.

I don't like how this all had to end,

For I am a woman who needs to be loved by her man.

It was such a perfect plan.

I want it all back again

Just the way it used to be,

With me and you.

(*Mmmm, to kiss you*),

This would be so wonderful to do.

STOP YOUR CRYING, AND WIPE YOUR EYES

I know the pain you're feeling right now,

But soon this time will pass somehow.

There is nothing wrong for a grown man to cry,

But save all those tears for when I die.

I'm only gone for a short while,

And for now we're living,

For how long, no one knows.

Time can be our best friend, or cause us much woe.

But soon time won't matter for you and I,

So I am asking you to do this, please.

Dry your eyes,

And please don't cry.

(*Stop your crying, and wipe your eyes*),

I know the hurt you're feeling inside,

But soon the pain will all be gone.

When you hear that knock upon your door and you go to answer it,

You'll see I'm home,

All your tears will finally be gone.

NO LAST CHANCE

He traced the lines upon her now-cold face, as he raptured her in his
warm embrace,

Thinking to himself of all the love he had missed in the years that had
vanished before him,

Like a cold, empty fog,

Remembering only that youthful love.

He had thought *the grass was much greener on the other side*,

As his now-broken heart felt the pang of guilt for betraying his once-
upon-a-time lovely bride.

As her lifeless body lay there in his trembling arms,

All he could think was,

"What went wrong?" after he had been gone from her presence for so
very long.

He remembered the night he packed his bags

And left,

As his young bride stood crying

And begging him not to go away,

Trying to persuade him to stay at least for one more day.

But as he was holding her now,

He realized it was all too late.

And remembering he was late for his date,

He had to be on his way before the hour of eight.

He knew at that moment as he continued to cradle her in his arms,

It was an awful mistake,

And all those memories in his heart he retraced,

As the warm tears streamed down his cheeks,

And landed on her now-cold face.

But his tears could not wake her now from her eternal sleep.

She had managed to maintain what he had left behind,

And from the look on her lifeless face,

The years had not been kind.

He was on his way back home to her that night,

Taking for granted everything would work out between them after all
       this time.

All he had to do was make it all seem right, attesting to all his wrong.

But God would not allow her any more pain, so he missed his last chance
       to hold her again.

Now in life did they part,

And it was not from suicide,

But simply from all those years of a broken heart.

When they came to take her body away, he glanced up at the ticking
    clock on the wall,

And the time was exactly eight,

And so for her *date*

She could not be late.

He suddenly realized

She had missed him for that last and final day.

WHEN THEY MET
A Short Story

The early evening sun was just beginning to sink into the unfathomable sea, hiding itself from the lovely full moon that would soon shine in the heavens for these *Virtual Lovers* like a spotlight shining on the two of them, and would soon be the center stage to perform all their dreams and fantasies. The cool ocean breeze would fan the flames of all their desires and a love that would only grow. All those long-awaited dreams and desires were about to come true for these two *Virtual Lovers*.

She never looked lovelier as she stood at the water's edge, gazing out into the distance with the light of love glowing from her emerald green eyes. A gentle breeze was blowing her long, brown hair, as it was whispering to her that her soul mate would soon be wrapping his arms around her waist.

He had been waiting and dreaming of this special moment for what seemed like a lifetime: the day he would meet his soul mate. She was everything that he had dreamed of. Without ever seeing her, he knew from that very first moment they had chatted in that small chat room several months earlier on the Internet, this was that special someone; as he would always say to her, *My Lady*.

Now, as he was driving to meet her, his mind was racing so fast with each beat of his heart, all that amazing, incredible love that he was holding inside for so long to give to her would soon unveil itself like the shroud falling from a master's work of art for all to see.

His gorgeous, blue eyes were radiant, so full of love, as he would behold her warm gracefulness, as he imagined her to be for so very long. That tender softness he felt in his dreams, night after night while lying in his bed, burning with flames of passion that only she could satisfy. This would be a moment made in heaven, and the angels were delivering it to them here on earth this very evening.

He anxiously searches for a parking space as he pulls into the hotel parking lot, looks in his rearview mirror, and sighs to himself, *Yes! This is the night.* He opens his car door, steps out of his car, his eyes searching the beach for her. All he can see in his mind is an image that had been created from a distinct description she had given him over the months they had chatted.

He walks at a fast pace, past the towering hotels that crowd the beach, casting their evening shadows on the white sand. All at once, his eyes fill with tears of amazement as he catches a glimpse of this beautiful figure standing there before him at the water's edge with her back to him, like they had planned. This was the way they wanted to meet for the first time.

She knows he is near. She senses his presence so close to her now. She sighs deeply, as a rush of passion fills her entire being. She feels him behind her. She hears his warm, soft moan as he gently slips his strong arms around her small waist, pulling her back so very tightly to his body from behind, nuzzles his face in her hair, his eyes closed, taking in the lovely smell of her hair. Raising one of his hands up and pushing her hair to one side of her head, exposing her ear, he lowers his mouth to her ear and slightly kisses it as he whispers in an accent, "I love you, my lady," and he sighs deeply.

She reaches down and takes his hands into hers and brings them up to her soft, moist lips, and kisses them ever so tenderly, still savoring the moment she would turn and look into his eyes for the first time.

He slowly turns her to face him, takes her small face into his hands as
their eyes meet for the first time, gazing longingly into each
others' eyes, caught in a moment of endless time, lost in each
others' eyes forever, their hungry mouths moving closer together
with each breath. As their lips meet, they both moan in deep
passion, their hearts now beating as one. They feel themselves
melting into one complete being. No more waiting, wondering;
they were finally together forever. Nothing would ever separate
them again, not even death. They had their whole lives ahead of
them now, and they both knew in that instant that it would be a
lifetime of happiness together.

Tears of happiness fill their eyes as they hold each other so very close.
They were at home, not like strangers; just so completely
satisfied.

He takes her soft hand into his and they leisurely take that long-awaited
walk on the beach, like they had dreamed of doing. No words
needed to be said.

He had once said to her during one of their many chats, "The Book of
Life has already been written. All we have to do is follow the
pages."

I PAINTED YOUR MEMORY

There is no canvas that my eyes can gaze upon you.

The colors of the paint I use are that of the human hue.

There is no frame that I can place your photograph in,

Except for the frame in my mind where we both have been.

Your memory I have painted of you, I shall not hang on a wall for others
to view,

But there is a place that I can go

To view all the memories of me and you.

It is hidden deep within my memory.

It lives on for as long as I do.

It can't be seen by others,

For I will not allow anyone to come inside to view.

But when they look through the windows of this now-barren soul,

They may see a glimpse of a story to be told,

For there they see the sadness of a long-ago happiness

That fate slowly stole.

I can see the look upon each that takes the time to see.

They wish to hear this story that has been hidden deep within me.

However, I fail to mention

Those who know my story of long ago,

Engraved into a reminiscence

Of lost tears that have failed to flow.

I hold back this mortal dam

Of the tears that were left behind,

Mixed with the salty waters of my tears

And a stale glass of sweet red wine.

I look at this canvas I have painted in mind,

At the most often times,

Like late at night with the moon all aglow,

With my conscious ablaze,

For it is your sweet memory that these weeping eyes wish to gaze,

For the memory of you, my pretentious love,

I shall never forget.

My Angel, My Song

You're my angel,

My song. You come to me like an angel, softly,

Tenderly,

Gently. I look into your heavenly eyes of blue,

And the first thought that comes to my mind:

"Oh God, how I love you."

You reach out your caressing arms to take me into our special heaven,

That place where there is no other but you and I.

That silent moment when the music of our souls starts to play that song
of heavenly bliss,

As I know I will soon be tasting the moistness of your angel kiss.

Our love meets in a place you and I cannot see,

But in a place where we can feel.

Your love brings with it

Music for my entire being.

We embrace to the sweet music we create from a tune within our hearts,
for this moment belongs to only you and I.

Mmmm, I hear you whisper to me,

I love you, baby, as we come together for that heavenly kiss.

You are truly my angel, my song.

CPSIA information can be obtained
at www.ICGtesting.com
Printed in the USA
LVHW071947010423
743236LV00002B/7